T0065433

DEATH AND THE KING'S GREY HAIR & OTHER PLAYS

DRAMA

Kraftgriots

Also in the series (DRAMA)

DEATH AND THE KING'S GREY HAIR & OTHER PLAYS

DRAMA

Denja Abdullahi

kraftgriots

Published by

Kraft Books Limited
6A Polytechnic Road, Sango, Ibadan
Box 22084, University of Ibadan Post Office
Ibadan, Oyo State, Nigeria
℡ 0803 348 2474, 0805 129 1191
E-mail: kraftbooks@yahoo.com

First published 2014

ISBN 978–978–918–166–7

= KRAFTGRIOTS =
(A literary imprint of Kraft Books Limited)

First printing, March 2014

Contents

Death and the King's Grey Hair

To the Oworo people whose dreams and aspirations eternally romance the confluence of the Niger and the Benue. One day, the spectre hovering over that lush land will give way ... the renaissance is at hand.

Author's Note

Inspiration came to write this play when I was an undergraduate at the university. It was at a Sociology class where we had to contend with the dynamics of various traditional African societies. The lecturer, himself looking rustic, made mention of an ethnic group, the Jukuns, in the Middle Belt Region of Nigeria, who in the ancient past never permitted their kings to grow old and feeble on the throne. At the first sprout of grey hairs, indicating ageing, the king has to take poison and die. His body is then taken to a sacred forest where it decomposes and is believed to be reborn as a lion.

This tradition at first appeared quaint to me but on a deeper reflection, I discovered the sense in it. Then came my conviction that most ancient traditions which modernity has taught us to regard as queer, really had a stabilizing role to play in the traditional community. After this conviction came my decision to use this ancient Jukun kingship tradition in a play, which shall dwell on power, its uses and its attendant problems in the human community. History has taught us that the attitude of the human community is yet to change with regards to power. Power, from the point of view of the primitive cave man, to the man of today's computer age, is the same. It may be argued that the human being, in terms of natural disposition, has never developed beyond his primordial essence; what is often called development is just a variation or fine-tuning of the timeless past.

The play is not a historical play for I have not conformed to any specific fact of history. What I have done is just to pick the bare thread of a fascinating tradition to serve as a base on which I wove an imaginative construct on power and the human community. This contention does not deny the play's borrowing from the diversity of the culturally rich traditional Africa.

Since the play does not lay a steadfast claim to a specific historical fact, the director is at liberty to subsume it under any traditional community when it comes to costume, songs, dances, and all other nuances of local colouring.

To end, I will reassert the dodged truth that much of the African past is still very relevant if we are interested in unravelling and demystifying the intricacies of the oppressive present.

Birnin Kebbi
October 1994

Dramatis Personae

King Esutu	–	The King of Shakaga
Royal Bard		
Gabisi	–	A poet and guardian of the word
1st Wiseman	–	The Chief Keeper
2nd Wiseman		
3rd Wiseman		
4th Wiseman		
5th Wiseman		
6th Wiseman		
7th Wiseman		
Inimisi	–	King Esutu's son
Prince	–	A visiting friend of King Esutu.
Man	–	Representative of the men
Woman	–	Representative of the women
Poison-Bearer		
Armed Men		
Youth	–	Gabisi's son

Drummers, dancers, maidens, royal retinue, flutist, guards and townspeople.

The play was first performed as the Kebbi State entry at the zonal stage (comprising Kebbi, Kano, Jigawa and Katsina States) of the NYSC Director General's Dance and Drama Competitions on the 3rd of October, 1995 at the Argungu International Fishing Festival Village in Argungu, Kebbi State. It was directed by Calvin Akaagerger.

Movement One

A sacred grove lights up on the stage. In the centre is an unwalled square-shaped hut with fresh palm leaves serving as a roof over thin woods. A poet sings the praises of seven sage-like men about to begin a deliberation. The poet is GABISI, *the poet of the sages in the land of Shakaga.*

GABISI: I am Gabisi, the poet of the ancients. Those who don't respect what is old should await the sting of my tongue. Wherever you see brave grey-haired men bent with many moons of wisdom, look for Gabisi. Gabisi is the messenger of tradition, the poet of the ancients.

Hail you seven wise men! I fear for the land when I see you gathered in this grove. Great and fearful things must be on their way to our land, for wise men like you never gather to tell jokes about women's behinds. That is for lustful young men whose loins are yet to father many children. From your fertile forge generations have been born. You hold the keys to the secret of our land. Those who want to know the land must pay you homage. With you wise men lies what makes us a race.

(The wise men have all along been nodding to the chant of GABISI. *Then, one of them raises his right hand.)*

1ST WISEMAN: That is enough, Gabisi. You are truly the poet of the ancient. You have always been with us. You and your offspring will continue to fraternize with this esteemed gathering, just like your ancestors. You said the truth. We do not gather to crack nuts like little children. But from time to time we gather to tie or untie the knots of tradition. You said you are the messenger of tradition?

GABISI: Yes, wise one.

1ST WISEMAN: Well, we sitting in this sacred grove are both the messengers and custodians of tradition.

GABISI: Your words can never be faulted.

1ST WISEMAN: And it is true that our gathering in this place foretells something important. Isn't it, elders of the land?

ALL: It is.

1ST WISEMAN: The time has come for us to tie the knots of tradition once again. We live by it and we shall die by it. The knot is about our king, King Esutu.

2ND WISEMAN: May he not live long!

1ST WISEMAN: That is how we salute kings in our land.

3RD WISEMAN: But this greeting seems to prolong Esutu's life.

1ST WISEMAN: You all know the footpath to the gourd of my words. As the chief keeper of our ancestral culture, I summoned this meeting because of Esutu's unusual long stay on the throne. We all know that it is a taboo for a king to show signs of ageing in our land. Our land is a land of young kings and short reigns. But something tells me that Esutu has stayed longer on the throne than any other king we've had since Jigulu, our founding father. The trees are asking, the wind is asking, the rivers are asking, the land is asking, the people are asking: why?

4TH WISEMAN: We all know where you are going, Chief Keeper. We have also asked ourselves several times before. That's what makes us the custodians of tradition. It is frightening to see the king outliving his subjects. Esutu's kingly face has stared too long at us and it is scaring our women and children. Esutu has the body of an ageing man but the hair of an uncircumcized boy.

5TH WISEMAN: I must enter the dancing square now, for

the man who refuses to dance in his wife's birth hole must expect to be disobeyed. Chief Keeper and everyone here know that it is the presence of grey hairs that terminates the rules of kings in our land. And I, Otolofon, am mandated by tradition to examine the king's head season by season. I have been doing this since the death of my father many moons ago. These two hands of mine have ruffled many royal heads in search of that terminal sign. With King Esutu, grey hairs seem to be afraid to appear. Every new season, I meet Esutu's head blacker than it was the season before.

7TH WISEMAN: Things of the old are about to fade away. I fear for what will happen to us the guardians of the land.

1ST WISEMAN: We are not here to lament, wise one. The land needs a new king if peace is to be kept. Esutu is gradually growing fangs of misrule because he has stayed for too long. When a woman stays in her husband's house for too long, she becomes a witch.

2ND WISEMAN: How do we catch a witch if not by the gods' anger or confession?

1ST WISEMAN: The gods have not spoken. But shall we wait for thunder before we take refuge from the rain?

6TH WISEMAN: Not at all. But the only sign of kingly transition has not been seen by Otolofon, the ruffler of royal heads. Do we take this as a sign that the gods are too happy with Esutu's rule or that someone is trying to block the passage of the river in times of rain?

3RD WISEMAN: That is impossible. Who can engage thunder in a lightning duel? Esutu is no child to wish to eat with the gods. And a king like other ones in the past cannot just be the gods' most beloved. Traditions and taboos must be kept!

1ST WISEMAN: That is the knot we are here to untie, and in untying that, we tie the shaking land more firmly to its root. The day the oracle pronounced Esutu as our new king, it did not tell us he will rule forever. As I said before, ours is a land of young kings and short reigns. Esutu has ruled and handled enormous powers for fifteen seasons, the longest in the history of our land. And surprisingly the sign for departure refuses to come ...

5TH WISEMAN: It comes blacker and blacker.

1ST WISEMAN: We cannot sit and smoke our pipes when unusual things happen in our land. We must solve this riddle. Esutu must assure us he is not blocking the course of tradition.

4TH WISEMAN: And who is that one that will tactlessly put his finger in the mouth of a snake?

1ST WISEMAN: Our snake cannot afford to be that vicious. We are the hands that feed the snake. Esutu has the power in which we also have a share. It is the wish of the land, the supreme, which we are here to protect. The ruffler of royal heads will pay a visit to King Esutu. He will be our emissary. He will ask Esutu our questions. He will again demand to see the royal head.

5TH WISEMAN: But I do that only once a season.

1ST WISEMAN: Unusual situation calls for unusual response, wise one. When you come back from the palace, we shall hear from you. We shall not touch that palace until this riddle is solved. Tell Esutu this. These are my words, wise men. Do I speak your minds?

All: You do, wise one!

(GABISI *sees that the wise ones are getting ready to leave. He shakes his staff at them and resumes his chants.*)

GABISI: Rise, o you wise ones. Make not much haste for the bones are tired from carrying the burden of the tribe for too long. The wise have spoken their minds, it is left for those with ears to listen, and ruffler of royal heads, it is you I call. The trees, the land, the rivers, the wind and the people have sent you. Be brave, be confident, for you have been sent to put the land where it should be. You have been sent so that we do not wake up one day and eat with our anus while horsewhips tear the flesh of our backs. Fear not. It is the person that sent a messenger that the messenger fears and not the one the message is meant for.

(The wise men rise in different postures of the aged. OTOLOFON, the 5TH WISEMAN and ruffler of royal heads, approaches GABISI and shakes his staff at him in reverence of his chants.)

GABISI: I am Gabisi, poet of the ancients, the guardian of the words ...

Light fades.

Movement Two

The palace of KING ESUTU *of the land of Shakaga in its awesome splendour. The paraphernalia therein indicates the abode of the symbol of political authority and the spiritual head of the tribe. A golden stool with a leopard skin covering is placed at the centre of the palace. A cowrie-decorated door links the palace's inner chambers to the court where the king receives visitors and deliberates with his chiefs. The palace messengers fan the stool awaiting the coming of the king. Two slave girls kneel at the left and right sides of the kingly stool facing each other. The royal flutist tests his flute with a sonorous tune meant to usher in the king. The* ROYAL BARD *suddenly bursts out from the inner chamber of the palace signifying the approach of the king. He faces the cowrie-laced door and begins ....*

ROYAL BARD: The lion hs left his den, the lion is on his way, all men and creatures must make way. Tell me the one who wants to share a footpath with a lion? Tell me the bold one who wants to stand shoulder to shoulder with our king? Who can wrestle with our ageless king? He who has routed many wisemen in the game of wisdom. He who has thrown many cats on the wrestling ground. Father of many children. Owner of a well-stocked harem. Beloved of the gods. Our king eats no more with men. That is for mere beings like us. Our king dines with spirits and the gods. He who disobeys the king disobeys the gods and he shall not be spared. Let the representative of the gods tread softly, for the ground might give way under his heavy feet. Tread softly, softly, my king, the day awaits your direction.

(The KING *appears clad in warrior-like attire. He is agile as a middle-aged man on the turn to old age. He has jet-*

black hair with a skullcap placed delicately on his head. He is clean-shaven with three tribal marks screened horizontally on both of his cheeks. He looks quizzically at the ROYAL BARD and round the court, then walks in a slow and dignified pace to the royal stool. He takes a moment's look at the slave girls and snaps his fingers. The slave girls quickly stand up and rush towards the inner chamber. The KING sits and the fanners begin fanning vigorously. He motions to the ROYAL BARD.)

KING ESUTU: Where are the chiefs, the wise men?

ROYAL BARD: Who knows what wisdom might have made them to keep the king waiting?

KING ESUTU: You are fond of attributing their shortcomings to wisdom. What wisdom is there in a king coming to a place of meeting before his chiefs?

ROYAL BARD: My king, know that they are bent with age, old men's bones sometimes become too stiff after a bad night's sleep.

KING ESUTU: I do not need your running mouth to teach me what to know. If the wise men are too old to respect and deliberate with the king, then let them sit and chew grinded meat in their homes.

ROYAL BARD: The day surely cannot face your displeasure.

KING ESUTU: Then let it go according to my wish. Let no arrogant wise man doubt my power.

(A shout of "oh king may you not live long" is heard at the entrance to the court. The FLUTIST picks up the wind, sensing the arrival of the wise men. OTOLOFON comes in squatting before the KING who along with the BARD show surprises at seeing OTOLOFON without the other wise men. OTOLOFON addresses the KING with profuse kingly greeting: "Oh King, may you not live long, may your race to join the ancestors be swift …".)

KING ESUTU: Enough of your curses or greetings. I don't know what to call them.

OTOLOFON: They are greetings and blessings according to tradition, King. And, King, will this be the first time you've heard these kingly greetings?

KING ESUTU: Rather I should ask if you are the only wise man left in the land. Where are the others or have they all joined the ancestors since the last time we met?

OTOLOFON: Not yet, King.

KING ESUTU: Oh, they feel too old and wise today to squat before the king or sit before him?

OTOLOFON: No one dares disrespect our king, yet no community dares disrespect the gods and the tradition; not even its king or wise men.

(ROYAL BARD *cuts in.*)

ROYAL BARD: Today's sun seems to have risen from the west, King. Be wary, for I can smell the pungent odour of ancient words.

KING ESUTU: Let the sun blaze forth its fury but the earth will never run away. Otolofon, speak, sit down and tell me why it is only you I see before me.

OTOLOFON: I choose to remain squatting, King. Heavy words hardly allow a man to sit down.

KING ESUTU: Stand on your head if you wish. As to the heavy words you claim to have, let me tell you that the horns can never be too heavy for the cow that bears them.

OTOLOFON: True words. Before you today I am the messenger of the wise men, the overseers of tradition. And I was sent forth with the backing that the messenger does not fear the one the message is meant for but it is the sender that should be feared.

ROYAL BARD: Be wary, Messenger, or haven't you heard of

that foolhardy sheep that was sent to tell the lion to leave the jungle?

OTOLOFON: Bard, tell that tale to the gathering of children. The tale I have to tell today is not for village urchins.

KING ESUTU: Let me hear him, Bard.

OTOLOFON: Oh, King, the wise men sent me to ask, the land sent me to ask, the people sent me to ask: If you or anyone is blocking the march of tradition. I was also asked to remind you of the pledge you made before climbing the throne. Our land is a land of short reigns and young kings. The land feels you've ruled for too long. And a king who rules for too long courts disasters into our land. According to our tradition, the glory of our kings lies in their being reborn as a lion after their reigns. King, these heavy questions must be answered if the wise men should return to the palace and peace to the land. Remember, King, remember ...

(*The scene changes into a time in the past, the time of the ascendancy of* KING ESUTU *to the throne of Shakaga. He is in an ancestral hut with all the seven wise men in attendance.* KING ESUTU *is looking young, defiant and holding stiff a spear in his left hand while the right holds a fluffy horsetail. The seven wise men crouch around him. The* 1ST WISEMAN *suddenly springs up and splashes liquid on the bare body of* KING ESUTU *who is naked from the navel up with a white cloth tied round his groin.*)

1ST WISEMAN: Esutu, Esutu, Esutu, I have splashed on you the liquid of greatness, the liquid of command, the liquid that makes you the viceroy of the gods on earth. You will be great as long as you obey the gods, you will be obeyed as long as you obey our gods and traditions. But remember our land is a land of young kings and short reigns. That is why I cannot splash on you the liquid of long life and long reign. In this land we greet kings with the saying "May you not live long" which is not a curse but a prayer for those who have attained greatness. Esutu, Esutu, Esutu, listen; listen to the voice of the land ...

(*The* 1ST WISEMAN *picks up three eggs from a nearby calabash and smashes them on the floor. Immediately, a guttural voice floats around. The wise men place their heads on the ground, leaving* ESUTU *in his steadfast posture.*)

VOICE: The land is a land of short reigns and young kings. The king must be young to rule the land with the blood of the young. The blood of the young shouts the blessings of the gods. Rule the land with your young blood and achieve. The old and the wise among you are there to guide the young. Esutu, may you not live long when you become king for a very long life on the throne makes a king a tyrant. Or a king becomes an old senile man abandoning the land to conflicts and usurpers. Esutu, at the sprout of the first white hair on your head, seen by the ruffler of royal heads, you must drink poison, die and be taken to the forest where you will join your ancestors as a lion. Esutu, pledge your acceptance of the laws.

ESUTU: I pledge that I will obey the laws ...

(*Scene changes back to the present with* OTOLOFON *still squatting before the king in the court. A high throaty laugh escapes from the* KING's *mouth.*)

KING ESUTU: Ah ah ah ah ... I now see what you foolish lot are up to. You've spent the days away from the palace to plot my downfall. Let me tell you one thing, even if the priest will suffer, it will never be in the presence of his acolytes. You've forgotten that I am the viceroy of the gods in this land, I can summon my wrath on any mortal.

OTOLOFON: My lord, that is as long as you obey the laws of the land and as long as the people obey you for that. No matter the power of a king, he becomes nothing when the people decide not to obey and respect him.

KING ESUTU: So, you and your wise lots have told the people

to cease to obey me?

OTOLOFON: No, King, we wise men cannot take such rash decision. We are only concerned to see that no one blocks the course of tradition.

KING ESUTU: Must I take poison and die before my time? Even before you see the sign? Are you all in a hurry to see me off this throne so that you can install another victim of yours? Tradition, tradition, tradition, do you think you know that tradition better than I do? Look, if you are so disappointed at not seeing the sign on me then why not go to the fireplace to get ashes to pour on my head?

OTOLOFON: King, nobody can force things to run before their time and neither can anybody delay them.

KING ESUTU: Then why this sudden haughty visit if you think nobody can force things? Today is not the time for your yearly play with my hair. It is still two moons away or have you been sent to do that?

OTOLOFON: Yes, and I hope the king will permit?

KING ESUTU: The king will never permit to be trifled with. Now, go tell your wise men that they should take care not to start what they cannot finish. Tell them to remind one another that I am the king and they are my subjects. Tell them I await their presence in this palace or fearful things will happen in this land. If they are now too old to come to the palace then let them know that wise men can be found anywhere. Age does not confer wisdom on everyman. We only say it does out of respect for the old. And you, no filthy finger shall touch my head except when it is time. Get up, go squat with your kind, and remember to give them my words.

(OTOLOFON *gets up with a sorrow-filled shake of the head. He pays his half-hearted respect to the* KING *before making for the exit. The* ROYAL BARD *interrupts his sedate steps with a piercing cry,* OTOLOFON *waits to hear him.)*

ROYAL BARD: Hail the king! Those who are not quick to anger must be bastards. So, let no man play with the tail of a lion. Let those who want to share a footpath with the lion be wary of the lion's strength. Messenger, tell the wise men that those who give the dog the lion's tail to play with are only calling for trouble, trouble, and more trouble.

Light fades.

Movement Three

Back at the grove. The wise men are in council, but this time around a section of the ordinary people of the land, men and women are with them. GABISI, the poet, shouts the praises of the wise men.

GABISI: When the aged and the wise no longer concern themselves with the affairs of the land, then tell me what good path that land can follow. The foolish ones wait for trouble to eat up half of the peace of the land before trying to break its stubborn neck. But the wise beat back its ugly head ever before it bares its venomous teeth. Otolofon, the one who visited the lion's den and came back unscathed, tell us the news from the palace.

1ST WISEMAN: Yes, Otolofon, tell us the response of the king to our questions and demands.

(OTOLOFON *gets up to address the council.*)

OTOLOFON: Wise men and people of the land, I greet you all. I delivered your message to the king like all faithful messengers. I told the king the fears of the people and reminded him of his pledge before ascending the throne. Hmm, fearful words came out of the king's mouth ...

GABISI: Tell us those words that can be more fearful than that of the angry people and their gods.

OTOLOFON: The king says he is a lion and no dog should dare trifle with his tail!

2ND WISEMAN: So we are dogs in the eyes of the king?

OTOLOFON: He said we should remember he is the gods' chosen one and that we are mere mortals. And that we should be careful not to start what we cannot finish. The

25

king closed his eyes and declared that before opening them, the wise men should come back to the palace with their tails between their legs ... or else they would be made to know that there exist wiser men in this land.

3RD WISEMAN: The dog that will perish in the bush will surely cease to hear the call of the hunter. Those whom the gods want to destroy they will first make mad.

OTOLOFON: I have not finished. The king refused to let me do what my ancestors did in seasons gone by and what I have been doing for so many seasons. He said my hands have been afflicted with temporary leprosy. And that it was not yet time for me to put my filthy fingers on his head. That is what I brought back on my back from the palace.

7TH WISEMAN: The words of the king are words from a head that does not think deep.

6TH WISEMAN: To me it is more of words from someone who has drunk too much from the many wells of power.

4TH WISEMAN: Such harsh and humiliating words must be met with courage and sanctions! It is time that branch of a king should be told that he cannot escape from his roots. The people, the land and the gods are the roots from which any king derives his power to rule! He must know this!

1ST WISEMAN: Let us not allow the rash talk and actions of another man becloud our reasoning. Elders, don't be moved to anger. The king nearly called us dogs but if he had gone down deep into his mind he would have known that he is the dog and we are the leash holding him in check. And like the leash that we are, we must be careful and firm lest we let free a mad dog to roam the land.

GABISI: Patience, my lords. Tempestuous anger and impulsive actions in the old are signs of the absence of wisdom and experience. And I know all you revered ones here cannot be called anything but wise and experienced.

1ST WISEMAN: Otolofon, we are happy that you delivered our message the way we sent you. We thank you for that. Anything unworthy the king has said to you is not on you alone but on us all and on the people of this land of Shakaga who made us the custodians of tradition. I am happy we have representations from the people here with us. They came to me just yesterday to ask if we elders will sit and watch evil befall this land. We shall now hear from them.

(*A man gets up to speak.*)

MAN: In the name of the people of this land, I greet you all, wise men of the land. I cannot forget to greet Gabisi, the poet of the ancients and tongue of tradition. We the people of the land greatly fear that that master of power, tyranny, is about to invade our land and stay for good. Things never witnessed in this land are beginning to be witnessed. Taking of farmers' land without notice and with no explanation, abduction of men and women, seizing of property, cruelty, crude display of power and all other evil things are done in the name of the king. We ask you, wise men, since when has tyranny being allowed in this land? Before my father died, he never told me that power-drunk kings ever ruled this land. These new things are strange to us for our land has never being conquered by our enemies. It is only in conquered lands that such evil deeds take place. Must we all sit down and allow the king to turn us into slaves in our own land?

2ND WISEMAN: That will never happen. Look, man, even before you started to speak, we knew where you were going. We are convinced you have said all that is on everybody's mind. Now let the mothers of our children speak.

WOMAN: With all the concerned voices of the women of this land, I salute you, the wise men, the poet and all the people in this place. The women of this land have never been known to sit in the kitchen and watch strange things happen to this land. Elders, you've heard from the men. Whatever affects the men is bound to affect the women. It is even the women who suffer most when evil descends on the land. It is their husbands and children that are killed or maimed in times of war or trouble. And most times, such confused times give room for the looting of their honour. The women have decided not to ululate for the king anymore because of the evil things that are being let loose in the land. The king should know that he cannot stand the anger of women. No power on earth can save that king born of a woman, who rules without paying homage to the mothers. Wise men, the women sent me to tell you to tell the king that he should beware that no weapon of violence or power can stand that which the gods have given to women. I shall say no more.

1ST WISEMAN: I pray that the springs of motherhood never dry up in our land. Men are the half of the land and women are the other half. Men possess the powers of the arms and with women lie that of the spirit of the mother earth. Woman, tell our mothers and mothers of our children that we shall not run away from the truth and we shall never leave our duty to this land undone. People, go in peace and let us take your anger to the king.

(MAN *and* WOMAN *lead the people out of the grove.*)

1ST WISEMAN: Fellow wise men, you've heard from the land. Troubled times like this call for going back to the past to find a potent force …

2ND WISEMAN: What potent force, or shall we take up arms against the king?

1ST WISEMAN: You did not allow me to finish. We cannot take up arms against the king. We are old men. And I don't think I can remember when last our people rose against their king.

3RD WISEMAN: How can that be when we've never had any king like the one we presently have?

1ST WISEMAN: We are war-like people but we do not fight wars against ourselves. We fight our enemies and it's been long since we've had cause to fight an enemy.

3RD WISEMAN: Long time of peace and bounty can make a king to think that the people have forgotten about the sacred rules of tradition.

OTOLOFON: I am surprised to see old men like you beating the drums of war. Must we declare war to rid the land of this tyrant, Esutu?

1ST WISEMAN: No one is calling for war. War is the fight against the outside enemy of the land. The fight against an evil in the land is not war but a call to guard the land from destruction. And we are guardians of the land.

6TH WISEMAN: We must remember in any decision we take that the leading warriors of the land are loyal to the king.

1ST WISEMAN: A group of warriors do not amount to an army. You have forgotten that it is in the laws of this land that the king shall never set the warriors of the land against the land. Warriors fight those savage tribes that might want to test the might of the land. If warriors dissipate their power fighting armless people of the land then what happens when war is brought to our doorstep by outsiders?

2ND WISEMAN: All this talk of war and warriors will make us forget the potent force you mentioned before.

1ST WISEMAN: May age not take your memory! Fellow wise men, you've forgotten that power given to us by tradition.

2ND WISEMAN: You mean the power to call on the oracle in times of trouble?

1ST WISEMAN: In our present case, we do one last thing before calling the oracle.

3RD WISEMAN: You mean the sending of the "banner of strong warning," the one usually sent before the declaration of war to a stubborn enemy?

1ST WISEMAN: May age not take away your memory!

4TH WISEMAN: Warning again? When do we stop warning and do something?

1ST WISEMAN: Remember Esutu is still the king. We only suspect he is obstructing the march of tradition. We have no proof yet. Until we have that proof or until we see grey hairs on his head, we cannot tell him to take poison and die and be reborn as a lion. We can only warn him to cut his growing fang of tyranny.

6TH WISEMAN: And who shall take this banner to the king?

7TH WISEMAN: Who else can do that better than Gabisi, the messenger of tradition?

1ST WISEMAN: It is only Gabisi that has been chosen by tradition to do that. Gabisi is the guardian of the word. Gabisi will tell the king that the people are tired of his ways. Gabisi is the bee that will sting out the truth hidden in the king's heart. Gabisi, the message is heavy but the faithful messenger is never known to groan under the weight of any message.

(GABISI *shakes his staff seven times at the wise men and flicks his flywhisk over his shoulder.*)

GABISI: I am Gabisi, the poet of the ancients, the deliverer of heavy messages. I run no errand for the idle or for the foolish. I run errands for wise men who are the wisdom of the land and the custodians of tradition. No message can be too heavy for me, for my shoulder is broad enough to carry the heavy words of our dear elders. The palace will tremble at the step of my feet. I will go with your warning with no fear. The crumb-eating dog fears to tell its master that he is a glutton. Gabisi is neither an eater of crumbs nor a dresser of lies. I will never fail to perform the duty of my ancestors. I am the guardian of the word. Let all those who close their eyes to tradition await the sting of my tongue. Let those truth-dodging ears await the force of my words. I am Gabisi, the poet of the ancients …

1ST WISEMAN: Elders, Gabisi is our worthy messenger. Let us move to the shrine and hand over the sacred banner to him with the necessary rituals.

(*Elders stand to move towards the shrine. GABISI leads the way shaking his staff now and then. Light fades.*)

Movement Four

At the king's palace with all the grandeur of court life but the king is in an agitated mood. With the king is a young man with a haughty bearing which immediately places him as the king's eldest son. The ROYAL BARD *stands at his post at the left hand side of the king fiddling with his whisk.* INIMISI, *the king's son, decides to break the silence.*

INIMISI: Father, may I ask where the stiff-boned wise men are?

KING ESUTU: It is a thing of joy to beget a son that takes after the father. A son that is not only satisfied with rolling lavishly in his father's sweat. Must I have a prodigal for a son?

INIMISI: Has my simple question stirred my father's vexed spirit today?

KING ESUTU: Inimisi, your only concern in this land is to use your privilege of being the king's eldest son to haughtily march through this land, confiscating things of pleasure anywhere it pleases you. My ears are already full of tales of the king's son who lives on seized pleasure ...

INIMISI: Father, I cannot understand you this morning, I ask after the wise men and ...

KING ESUTU: For some stretch of time now the wise men have refused to stoop before the king. But the mighty son of the king has all along being engrossed in brew and sleeping far beyond cockcrow amidst women with easy thighs. Son, do you think I don't know that your harem is threatening to grow in numbers ahead of mine?

(*The* ROYAL BARD *interjects before* INIMISI *can get himself ready for a reply.*)

ROYAL BARD: Hail the king! Look with eyes of pride on your son and remember that that which the lion bore must be like the lion. Inimisi, give the king the ears of obedience. Remember that a young man's array of gorgeous cloths might equal or be more than those of the old man, but can that young man claim to have enough rags as those of the old man? King, if kingship succession in this land is from father to son, then I have no fear of Inimisi succeeding you.

KING ESUTU: What does he know other than drinking and watching the brimming rears of the women in his harem?

ROYAL BARD: He shall come to know, King. Let the young swim in the sweet streams of their youth for now ....

INIMISI: Am I to be the subject of exchange between you and the bard? I will leave if your vexed mood will spoil the day for me.

KING ESUTU: Leave, prodigal son! Leave to enjoy the spoils of war in which you never fought. Treachery will soon block the flow of the river that irrigates your pleasure field. The people plan evil against the throne and all my son does is drink, drink and ...

INIMISI: Father, leave me to my drink, but tell me are the wise men with them too?

KING ESUTU: Too many moments spent in the embrace of women with fish-like brains has made my son soft in the head. Who else? Tell me who else will be behind the plot of the people if not the so-called wise men. Softhead, don't you know that the refusal of the wise men to come before the king is the beginning of treachery?

INIMISI: I have had enough of this name-calling! You have already spoiled the day for me with your misplaced anger. Now to repair the spoilt day, I must taste the sweetness coming from the top of the tree of life, the palm. (*He grins in anticipation.*) Father, you need to increase your intake of the fluid from the tree of life. More and more fluid from the tree of life will calm you against all treachery ... ah ah ah. Hurrah to the palm! (*He runs out with a leap.*)

KING ESUTU: Accursed be the day you came into this world, you drunkard! The palm that you worship will receive your bloated body, for you shall drown in its fluid ...

ROYAL BARD: Patience, my lord. He knows not what he is doing. Leave him to his wines. He will be back in the gathering of the sane when the tree he worships dries up.

KING ESUTU: Are you saying my son is mad?

ROYAL BARD: Turn not your anger against me, King. Who am I to glare into the blazing eye of the sky? The tale that the king's wife is a witch will not be heard from my mouth. Your son is not mad, King, but too much drink can make a sane man bring out his leaking penis in the market square. Then what do we call such a person?

KING ESUTU: Mad!

ROYAL BARD: So says the king. (*Smarts.*) King, I think I can hear drums, drums beating the tunes of a faraway land.

(*The* KING *strains his ears and picks faint echoes of vigorous drumbeats backstage. He grins as he recognizes the origin of the beats. He springs up and slowly sways to the approaching beats with the bard looking on admiringly and in bewilderment.*)

ROYAL BARD: King, what can bring such sudden happiness after a vexed morning talk of treachery and drunkenness?

(*The king stops and casts a glance at the bard.*)

KING ESUTU: Fool! Have you forgotten my friend the Prince of the land beyond the great river? My friend, the prince, who has never failed to visit me every two seasons since I became king of this land. Let me dance to welcome my friend.

(He continues to sway and the drumbeats get nearer and nearer till the sudden entry of five men bedecked in soldierly attire and vigorously dancing to the drumming. Young maidens make their entry with equally vigorous dance steps and hotly pursued by the drummers. Then, as if from a cue, the drummers change the beat of the drums to that of a mellifluous tune; the maidens form a circle and start an opening song.)

Ejadeee kẹwa wo wao x2	Come out and observe us
Nigbatawa balo tan	So that you don't argue
Koma dariyan jiyan	Among yourselves when we are gone
Ejadeee kẹwa wo wa o	Come out and observe us

(Any other song of opening, making a clarion call will do. See appendix.)

(In the middle of the maidens' performance, young men and women carrying varied bundles on them come in. Amidst the load carriers is a tall, well-built man, richly decked in flowing Aso-Oke and beads. He waves a horsetail in his right hand and gently sways to the maidens' tune with the carriage of someone important. The man, all smiles, leaves the midst of the load carriers and moves to the inside of the circle formed by the maidens. He dances around them and playfully taps their behinds with his horsetail. Then raising his head he sees KING ESUTU smiling at the spectacle before him. He leaves the circle and dances towards him. KING ESUTU also gracefully dances towards his friend. They meet and embrace. The visiting man raises his horsetail and halts the wedlock of swaying bodies and throbbing drums.)

KING ESUTU: Welcome, my friend from the land beyond the great river. You've brought joy into my heart with your visit, just when treachery is about to drive joy out of the land.

PRINCE: Have I come in time of war or serious grief? Tell me, have I set a wrong foot on this land?

KING ESUTU: My friend, forgive me if I met your joy with words that drip of grief. I know you to come always before the onset of a feast or right in the middle of it. May you never enter a land in a time of sorrow. Let joy always welcome you wherever you go.

ALL: Ase!

KING ESUTU: My dear friend, do you come a prince or a king like me, for I can see signs of kingship in your grand entrance.

PRINCE: The Prince is still before you. The old man is in love with this earth. He is not in a hurry to leave. We have had periods of bounties in our land since the last time I came here and that is what you are seeing!

KING ESUTU: Be you Prince or King, a Prince like you is a King in waiting; waiting to ascend the throne of your forefathers. May it be so.

ALL: Ase!

KING ESUTU: I must also show that this land never lacks a way to warmly welcome a great friend and visitor like you. Bard, call out those who give joy, tell them to come welcome my friend. Take the Prince's followers to their place of rest and tell my women to give them enough of all things good.

(*The bard leaves with the Prince's followers into the inner chambers of the palace. The king's entertainers arrive with a song of welcome preceding them. (See appendix.) They entertain the king and his visitor with their repertoire of*

songs and dances. The entertainers leave and the ROYAL
BARD *places a big keg of palm wine before the King and his
visitor. The Bard pours the wine into the calabashes,
handing one to the King and the other to the Prince. They
take a long draught and smack their lips in satisfaction.)*

KING ESUTU: Prince, the taste of friendship lingers in the
mouth like a bitter kolanut.

PRINCE: And it is stronger than the taste of this wine before
us.

KING ESUTU: Two thousand needles do not amount to an
axe, one thousand stars do not shine like the moon, and
the loyalty of two thousand servants does not compensate
for the absence of a true friend.

PRINCE: Wise words, King. True friendship like lost virginity
can never be undone.

KING ESUTU: The king is bereft of friends in his own land.
Even the King does not need friends to rule the land. His
is to command and his subjects are to obey. But what do
we say of toothless old men who teach village urchins
how to beat the drums of malice against the king? Are
they friends or enemies?

PRINCE: In my land, such toothless heads are detached from
their foul bodies before the shrine of the Iron-god. But,
King, what is this talk of toothless old men urging village
urchins to treachery?

KING ESUTU: My friend, my chiefs, the wise men, have
vowed not to step into the palace until I show them that
I have not been obstructing the march of tradition.

PRINCE: Why?

KING ESUTU: They are envious of my long reign.

PRINCE: The long reign of a good king is a blessing to any
land. Are your people afraid of a king reigning for long?

KING ESUTU: Our land is a land of young kings and short reigns. My friend, you talk as if you have never heard the way the wise men do greet me.

PRINCE: Ah! I remember they place a curse and say it is greetings. "May you die soon" or what is it they used to say?

KING ESUTU: No, they say, "May you not live long."

PRINCE: And what is the difference between dying soon and not living long? Such strange greetings to the head that wears the crown? In my place, you must pray for the king to live long until his mouth is bereft of teeth. Even if you want the king dead, you dare not say it or your head would grace the shrine of the iron-god. Tell me, King, do the wise men want your throne?

KING ESUTU: None of them is fit to ascend this throne unless chosen by the oracle. They've sent their messenger to express their surprise at my unusually long reign.

PRINCE: You call your ten seasons, or so, on the throne a long reign? Do you know that my father, the great king of the land beyond the great river has been there for thirty seasons? And yet people fawn over themselves praying for him to rule for years longer than the previous.

KING ESUTU: Our ways are different from yours.

PRINCE: Now that they feel you've stayed too long, what exactly do they want to do?

KING ESUTU: The sign of ageing detected by the ruffler of royal heads, one of the wise men, carries the verdict of death on the reigning king. But to the surprise of those envious lots, I am not in a hurry to age.

PRINCE: Why should you be before it is your time, when you have a brimming harem to contend with? Oh! King, I have brought another juicy virgin to keep you busy.

KING ESUTU: I know you not to forget such gift. Just wait to see the treasure you will go home with.

PRINCE: Forget all treasures and just hand me one of the women with flowing rears that are about in your land ... (ROYAL BARD *cuts in.*)

ROYAL BARD: Red feathers are the pride of the parrot;
Young leaves are the pride of the palm tree;
White flowers are the pride of cotton;
A straight tree is the pride of the forest;
A fast antelope is the pride of the bush;
The rainbow is the pride of heaven;
A beautiful woman is the pride of her husband;
And all things good and pleasurable are the pride of kings and men of might like you.

PRINCE: You are right, Bard! I remember my father's bard once chanted that:
Great beauty that moves the hearts and loins are for:
The farmers with the heftiest yams;
For warriors with the sharpest swords;
For medicine men with the most potent charms;
For randy men with the most infectious smiles;
Palace guards! Hasten to the houses of that wretched man
Who houses that beautiful woman with the trembling thighs.
Tell him that he has committed a crime by sleeping with such a beautiful woman, in a land where there is a king!

ROYAL BARD: I said it before, all good things are for men of power and might such as our king and his good friend, the Prince.

KING ESUTU: Before we get lost in the joys of all things good, tell me, friend, do you come with my ageless gift?

(PRINCE *starts to smile like someone recollecting something nearly forgotten.*)

PRINCE: I never forget whatever can bring joy to my good

old king.

KING ESUTU: Let us enter then to commune with the harbinger of everlasting youth.

(*Exit* KING ESUTU *and* PRINCE *just as* GABISI *the poet of the ancients makes his entry holding a long stalk draped with a black piece of cloth. The* ROYAL BARD *takes in the spectacle and prepares for a challenge.* GABISI *briefly regards the bard condescendingly and then glares at the entrance to the inner chamber of the palace.*)

ROYAL BARD: And what gives a dog the courage to step into the lion's den?

GABISI: The lion roams round the bush and picks on animals to feed on at will. All is through the grace of the earth. But the day the earth rises against the lion, its tails will be a plaything of the dogs.

ROYAL BARD: Such insolence! Haven't you heard that there can be no peace wherever the lion's tail is given to the dogs to play with?

GABISI: Who talks of a bastard peace when honour, tradition and justice are being trifled with?

ROYAL BARD: By who? And are you the person sent to put all things in place? And what is that mournful thing in your hand?

GABISI: Your eyes have been too much around sights of ease to recognize signs of unease in the land. This is the banner of warning. This banner carries the people's voice that the king should submit to the people's question or face the wrath of the land. If your shallow memory permits, think and you will remember that this banner precedes our warriors to the land where we are about to make war.

ROYAL BARD: So, you and your clan of dogs and flies want to make war with the king? Let it be known that a whole clan of flies cannot push over a cow.

GABISI: But the same flies will live to tell the tale of the fallen cow. The gnat might not be fit enough to clothe the giant, but it can make the giant fling away his trousers, right in the marketplace.

ROYAL BARD: Do you think our king is like pounded yam that you can mould in your hand? You lie! You can never play with the lion cub. You think you can carry your insulting mouth wherever it pleases you? Wait and you will soon know that our king is like a buffalo that makes the hunter to vow not to hunt again. When the king finishes with you, you will never think of taking your mouth beyond the huts of those toothless old men you call wise.

GABISI: Must I suffer indignities in the hand of a descendant of palace slaves, eaters of crumbs and impotent repeaters of shallow praises? I don't blame you; you are like a dog that follows its master though it does not know where he is going. I came here to talk to the king and hence I will speak not until the king comes.

(*The* ROYAL BARD *is now enraged.*)

ROYAL BARD: Wait! Wait to be scalded by the king's fire. A commoner like you, defiling this noble abode with your rotten breath! Wait and with your wretched strong head, look the sun in the eye. You will leave here blind. I promise you that.

(*Just then, the* KING *emerges, looking intently at a mirror held close to his face. He pats his hair and turns to the* PRINCE *who all the while is smiling. The* ROYAL BARD *brings them out of their private world of reverie.*)

ROYAL BARD: Oh King, in the absence of the cat, the mouse walked confidently in the house of the swift-footed one.

(*The* KING *spins round and sees* GABISI, *who at the same time raises the staff in greeting to the king.*)

GABISI: Oh King, may you not live long, and may your race to get reborn as a lion be swift!

PRINCE: This awful greeting again! King, why not decree this greeting out of existence?

GABISI: Stranger, when things of the house are being discussed, a sensible stranger never interferes until he is called upon.

KING ESUTU: And who are you to call my friend a stranger to this land? The treacherous loyalty of a thousand like you never amounts to the smallest support of a good friend like the Prince.

GABISI: King, enjoy the deceptive colour of friendship but know that those that are truly your friends have sent me to you.

KING ESUTU: What friends do I have left in this land where the wisest have turned to snakes whispering evil to willing ears?

GABISI: The wise men remain the most loyal to the land and its ways. I have in my left hand something that you know very much.

KING ESUTU: Such audacity! A warning from my subjects? A warning about what?

GABISI: The people, the land want you to submit to their total enquiry. King, you've ruled us for too long, so says the people and the fang of tyranny is daily stinging the heels of the people. They want you to prove that you have not been blocking the course of tradition.

KING ESUTU: And how do I prove that?

GABISI: King, you must come to the grove and submit yourself to a divination ritual of the wise men, after which you will be taken to the marketplace where the wise men will put the matter arising from the divination to the people. The people will then ask questions and you will answer.

KING ESUTU: And what if I refuse to be ordered around by my subjects ...?

GABISI: Then I fear for the land.

PRINCE: Who is the commoner with the sheepish courage to tell the King what to do?

ROYAL BARD: He is the praise-singer of those toothless old men called wise men.

GABISI: I am Gabisi. I am nobody's praise-singer. I am a poet of the ancients, the guardian of the word, the nib in the pond of silence, the scourge of all those who depart from the land and the people.

KING ESUTU: Let it be known that I, King Esutu of the land of Shakaga, I am the terrible scourge of all those who disrespect constituted authority. Have you forgotten that the king is next to the gods and all must stoop before him or be destroyed?

GABISI: That is true as long as the king rules according to the dictates of the tradition, of the laws of the gods. The moment the king does otherwise, then I fear such power no longer exists.

KING ESUTU: Enough is enough! I must show people like you that I am still the king of this land and I will continue to be king as long as no white hair is found on my head ...

GABISI: That alone is not enough ...

KING ESUTU: Don't take words away from my mouth. You rejoice in the liberty given to you to spread your saliva all over the land.

GABISI: The freedom to speak the truth is given by the gods, not by any man.

KING ESUTU: It is time that freedom to spread abuse, malice and treachery is taken away from you and people like you. I have no message for those that have sent you and so you will remain here under watch, for you are like a rabid dog that can poison the whole land if left to roam free.

GABISI: King, too much power is intoxicating and I can see the signs of the drunk in you.

KING ESUTU: Me? Drunk?

PRINCE: This wretched man deserves to be beheaded before the shrine of the iron-god. It is the person who disrespects the king that the king kills.

KING ESUTU: Bard, call me the palace guards to take this dung away from me and hide him in the darkest of holes.

(*Bard rushes out and comes back with two armed guards who seize* GABISI *violently, but* GABISI *still holds aloft the banner of warning pointing it accusingly at the* KING *as he is being dragged away.*)

GABISI: Power-drunk-king, you can never imprison the word! The word will always outlive the palace! The people will outlive you! No matter what, the truth shall prevail!

(*Light fades as* GABISI *curses the* KING *and struggles with his captors.*)

Movement Five

(Back at the grove, sit the seven wisemen in deliberation over the new turn of things in the land.)

1ST WISEMAN: What we fear has come to happen. The King has chosen to imprison the word. Gabisi has been detained. What further proof do we need to know that the King is surely blocking the course of tradition?

2ND WISEMAN: The King must be challenged!

4TH WISEMAN: For how long will this challenge be made without a fight?

OTOLOFON: From what I've seen so far, I know this matter will not die with the land remaining the same.

1ST WISEMAN: The land will not die because of the madness of one man. Kings come and go but the land always remains.

7TH WISEMAN: What do we do next?

2ND WISEMAN: The poison bearer must visit the King.

OTOLOFON: When the grey hair is yet to be spotted on the King's head?

2ND WISEMAN: I have a feeling that we shall be below the ground before that grey hair appears.

OTOLOFON: All the same, tradition says the grey hair must come before a king is asked to leave.

2ND WISEMAN: But there must be a way out of this trouble.

1ST WISEMAN: The way out is what we should calm down to find. The truth is that we must not allow things to continue this way.

(*Out of nowhere a man bursts on to the deliberating wise men, panting.*)

1ST WISEMAN: What gives you the boldness to jump on us when we are at this sacred place? Have you been sent by the King to kill us?

MAN: Forgive me, wise ones, I have an urgent message that cannot wait ... I have been running from the last village at the boundary of the great river.

2ND WISEMAN: Should we bring you water then?

MAN: Wise one, no water can quench the urgency of the message I bring.

1ST WISEMAN: Then let us hear.

MAN: I met the king's visitor in the tapper's compound with his entourage on their way to their land, drinking and dancing.

6TH WISEMAN: Trust that prodigal prince to worship his leisure god at any moment and at any place.

MAN: No one quarrels with a man for reveling in the joys within his reach, so say you wise ones, but I heard a thing from that man's mouth that I could not understand.

1ST WISEMAN: Tell us, for it is the job of the wise to give advice on things that are not known to the ordinary man.

MAN: The king's visitor, after too much wine, boasted to the tapper that he has with him the ageless gift, which he gives the king whenever he visits our land.

OTOLOFON: Ageless gift? What can that be?

MAN: As soon as I heard that he gives the king an ageless gift, I ran to let you know.

1ST WISEMAN: There's no time to waste. Otolofon, get some armed men to follow this man and let that depraved prince be seized along with all that are with him and let them be brought here.

Light fades.

(*At the grove again. This scene should be mimed with drums, flutes, gestures that rhyme with the trend of actions. The atmosphere is tense as the wise men await the men that had been sent to bring the* PRINCE. *Soon the* PRINCE *is led in with his followers. He maintains his regal and haughty mien in spite of being ruffled by the armed men. The wise men, in inquisitive gestures, demand to know what had transpired between him and the King. After a period of silence and agitated promptings, the* PRINCE *brings out a pouch from the folds of his big gown and dangles it before the wise men, smiling and praising the efficacy of its content. He opens it and takes out a handful of a black powder, demands for a calabash of water and empties the handful into it. He stirs the mixture, and then beckons on one of the wise men. The bewildered wise man approaches. The* PRINCE *raises up the calabash containing the now black solution and pours some on the grey hair of the wise man. Immediately all the grey hair on the wise man's head turn to deep black. The* PRINCE *beckons on the other wise men to examine the transformation.* OTOLOFON *leads the pack of examiners. Each examination elicits a vigorous shake of the head by the examiner. At the end, a look from the first wise man sends the armed men seizing the* PRINCE *once again and leading him and the entourage away from the grove. The gestures by the wise men indicate that the* PRINCE *and followers should be escorted with dispatch out of Shakaga and beyond. A comely maiden among the entourage, a dash from* KING ESUTU, *is made to stay behind. The* PRINCE *turns round to protest but he is forced away. The maiden now picks a broom to sweep the feet of the* PRINCE *and followers out of the land.*)

Light fades.

(*Light comes on to reveal the grove again. This scene is mimed with mournful notes coming from the drums and flute. OTOLOFON appears in front of a line of the wise men holding a black calabash. Just then, a figure appears in the opposite direction making his way towards the wise men. The figure is draped in red loincloth and has a clean-shaven head. He is the traditional POISON-BEARER, usually sent to a king whose time is up. The king is expected to take the poison in the calabash and die so that he can be reborn as a lion in the sacred forest. OTOLOFON hands over the calabash to the POISON-BEARER and a dirge is started to go with the mournful notes from the drums and flute. The POISON-BEARER turns away from the wise men with the calabash sitting on his outstretched palms. He takes sedate steps that conform with the chorus of the dirge as he moves from the grove with the stationary wise men watching his retreating figure. See appendix for dirge.*)

Light fades.

Movement Six

(*At the king's palace. The* KING *enters with the* ROYAL BARD *and* INIMISI *trails drunkenly behind them.*)

ROYAL BARD: My king, the departure of your friend seems to have enlivened your spirit rather than dampen it.

KING ESUTU: My friend, the Prince, is like the rain to a long famished land. His coming gives joy and joy remains long after he has left. I am refreshed, I am rejuvenated, I am ready now to take on those childish old men and their accomplices.

ROYAL BARD: (*Addressing the king's son who still stands swaying drunkenly.*) Inimisi, let the spirit of rejuvenation oozing out of the King clear the fumes of the palm from your head. Forget this ceaseless worship of the pleasurable things of life and with the King, face the adversaries.

INIMISI: I hear you, Royal Bard, but I have been seduced by the palm, the potent brew and all the good that flows from it. If I am to turn, it can't be sudden, it must be gradual, gradual and gradual ...

KING ESUTU: Leave him, Bard! The dog that will get lost will never hear the whistle of the hunter.

INIMISI: Let the hunter find another dog and let the dog go hunting alone, drink alone, eat alone and alone it will mate with its kind.

(*Suddenly a solemn tune wafts into the palace. Soon the tune gets to be heard as the same dirge notes that accompanied the poison-bearer out of the grove. They listen intently to make out its meaning.*)

ROYAL BARD: King, I can hear tunes that sing of farewell to the land of the living.

KING ESUTU: Who dares bring the song of death to my palace? This drum of treachery has beaten for too long to be ignored! Inimisi, call for the palace guards and soldiers.

(INIMISI *staggers out of the court and the* POISON-BEARER *emerges with his sedate steps, conforming to the dirge song and the calabash is aloft.*)

ROYAL BARD: Ah! Here comes the poison-bearer. His coming, King, says you must take poison and die ...

KING ESUTU: Take poison and die? To die when it is not time? Where is the ruffler of royal heads? Let him come to do his job.

(*The silent* POISON-BEARER *opens his mouth to speak and the dirge song stops.*)

POISON-BEARER: What was hidden has been exposed. The stranger Prince was accosted on his way out of our land and before the wise men, he exposed what has long been hidden. I bring you poison, King, I bring you honour, take this poison, die and get reborn as a lion in the sacred forest. That is the price of kingship.

KING ESUTU: No! I reject your suicidal honour. What honour lies in dying by one's own hand to come back as a common animal?

POISON-BEARER: That is the way of our people ...

KING ESUTU: That way must change for I will not take your poison ... you will take that poison yourself and if you like, get reborn a dog. You must have a taste of your own medicine. Guards!

(*The guards rush in and, at the king's command, they seize the immobile* POISON-BEARER, *stretch him on the ground and empty the contents of the calabash into his mouth. The*

ROYAL BARD *looks at the prostrate figure of the* POISON-BEARER *and shakes his head.*)

ROYAL BARD: The poison-bearer has been made to taste the instant death in his own poison. Things unheard of have happened and we shall soon be seeing things that have never been seen.

KING ESUTU: Bard, did I hear you well? Remember the house bird does not eat and drink with the owner of the house only to fly away on the day of death.

ROYAL BARD: I am with you, King, but it is just that I can smell war and fearful things on their slow but steady approach to the palace.

KING ESUTU: Must we remain to get engulfed by their treachery? Look, the toad likes water but not when it is boiling. We must leave this land and find fortunes in other places. Guards! Prepare the horses and everybody. We must take flight before sunrise. Before I forget, take out that mad poet and kill him!

(*Some guards rush away while others stand guard beside the* KING.)

KING ESUTU: Bard, get ready too.

ROYAL BARD: Where else will a court poet like me practise his trade if not the palace? My father and my father's father have known no place but this court. I will not flee from my place of duty.

KING ESUTU: You son of crumb-eaters! You want to eat more crumbs after I am out of here? No way! Guards, seize him! Let him die with his friend, the mad poet.

(*The guards seize the* ROYAL BARD *as he tries to get away. He hurls abuses at the king as he is being dragged away.*)

ROYAL BARD: Coward King! Wherever you go, you will know no peace! Your evil name will be erased from the memories of men! You will die a shameful death ...

(*Light fades as the* BARD *is dragged out and the* KING *rushes out of the court.*)

Movement Seven

Light comes on to reveal the palace grounds on the morning after the flight of the king at dawn. Numerous armed men burst into the court chanting war songs and are followed by the ordinary people: men, women, young and old, holding sticks and weapons of assault. The seven wise men bring up the rear. The armed men charge into the inner precincts of the palace while the people and the wise men wait in the court. The armed men re-enter the court carrying high three lifeless forms. Silence descends on the hitherto agitated crowd.

1ST ARMED MAN: Wise ones and people, we came too late. It seems the King fled just before dawn.

2ND ARMED MAN: And these are the bodies we found dumped inside one of the palace rooms. The wounds on two are fresh and the third one has no wound.

(1ST WISEMAN clears the way and approaches the bodies now lying on the ground.)

1ST WISEMAN: Ah! This is Gabisi; the guardian of the word has been felled by the tyrant's sword.

(The women begin to wail.)

1ST WISEMAN: Hold it! Women, this is no time for wailing. This is the body of the dog, the Royal Bard. He must have refused to flee with his master and has been killed in anger. And this is the poison-bearer, obviously forced to take the poison he was sent to give the King. These deaths and the King's flight mark new beginnings in our land.

A VOICE FROM THE CROWD: Let us give them a hot chase before they go too far

ALL: Yes. Let's go!!

1ST WISEMAN: No use, great people. Let him flee to his doom. He flees with all that is wrong with our land. Our land shall now breathe fresh air for the King's flight signifies the fleeing of the oppressive days we've been experiencing so far.

ANOTHER VOICE FROM THE CROWD: We will welcome no king in this land again!

ALL: We agree!

OTOLOFON: This horrible disregard for tradition by the accursed King might be the god's way of telling us to crown no more king in this land.

2ND WISEMAN: Power shall no longer be placed in the hands of one man.

4TH WISEMAN: When a way of doing things no longer agrees with the feelings of the day, then it is time for it to be discarded. Away with kings and their likes!

1ST ARMED MAN: And away with the Royal Bard, the royal children, the royal harem and all other royal privileges seized from the people's hands!

2ND ARMED MAN: What do we need a haughty and rotten king for, when there are wise people to guide the land?

ALL: Yes, the land should be placed in the hands of the wise men!

6TH WISEMAN: Chief Keeper, speak! Speak for the people have placed their trust in us.

1ST WISEMAN: Greetings to you all in the name of this decisive moment in the history of our land. You have, with no argument, placed the affairs of the land in our hands. The land belongs to you and we will only manage it the way every loyal servant manages the things placed in his trust by his master. We will not manage with the giddy head of one man. Whatever we do will be with togetherness and with the anxiety to conform to your wishes. The wand of our status has never been passed from father to son and it will remain so. If we make a mistake, you have every right to call us to order, for you are the owners of all that we attend to.

OTOLOFON: On behalf of the wise men, I give our pledge of selfless service.

ALL: We accept!

1ST WISEMAN: Now let us honour the honourable ones that died in the process of cleansing the land. The land soiled by tyranny. First, Gabisi must not die unsung. Gabisi was the guardian of the word, the lifter of the banner of truth. Take him and bury him with all the rites befitting the great. We will have three full evenings of songs, dances and plays in his honour. Gabisi has a son I think ... where is he?

(*A youth emerges with assured steps from the crowd.*)

You are Gabisi's son?

YOUTH: Yes, wise one.

1ST WISEMAN: It is said that when the fire dies, it covers itself with ashes and when the banana tree dies, it replaces itself with an offshoot. Gabisi died honourably and you, as the eldest son, should continue from where he stopped. You are the new lifter of the banner of truth, the scourge of deceptive beings, the possessor of the scalding tongue, the inheritor of the ancient words, the weaver of sweet and sensible songs, and the utmost guardian of the word. Son, pick up the banner and do the job of your ancestors.

(*The youth picks the banner beside the body of* GABISI. *The armed men carry* GABISI *away for the burial rites.*)

1ST WISEMAN: The poison-bearer is a fearless messenger. Let him be given the burial of the brave and let him be rewarded as the one that gave the final push to tyranny out of our land.

(*The body of the* POISON-BEARER *is taken away.*)

Now we are left with the body of the impotent repeater of shallow praises. His type will never be seen in this land again. It is only where there is a court that we can find a court fool like him. Our land shall no longer welcome a royal court, so there will be no court poet. Let the royal fool be buried like a dog that he was in life. No one should weep for him.

(*The* ROYAL BARD's *body is dragged on the floor to his place of burial.*)

Now, son of Gabisi, give us words of courage to face this new beginning.

SON OF GABISI: The battle may rage with mountains of death
But someone will always remain to tell the story.
After all is said and done,
The word will remain to outlive all things.
Wisdom is the pride of man;
A land in the hands of the wise
Shall never go astray.
Those entrusted with power
Should not get drunk from its fumes
Those who are not with it
Should watch with wide-opened eyes
The people will always outlive all evils.

Beat the gong with festive frenzy;
Blow the trumpet to high heaven.
Caress the drum like a fond friend;
Call the flutist to commune with the wind.
Mark this end, mark this beginning.

(*At this, the people file out of the palace along with the wise men, with songs of a new beginning. The song chosen should be that which is not overtly joyous nor dirge-like. It should capture the mood of marking a not too happy end and a* beginning that gives the promise of a prosperous time ahead only after surmounting great obstacles *(see appendix). Light fades.)*

Curtain.

APPENDIX

Song One

ẹjadeee kẹ wa wo wao x2	Come out and observe us
nigbatawa balọ tan	So that you don't argue
Koma dariyan	Among yourselves when we
jiyan	are gone
ẹjadeee Kẹwa wo wao etc.	Come out and observe us etc.

Song Two

Abamisayọ ye abamisayọ	Rejoice with me, rejoice with me
Ẹyẹ gbogbogi abalogo sayaya	Come all birds and share this sweet song
Ile ẹlemọni abaya sayọ	The grove should join in this joy
Ẹyẹ gbogbogi abalogo sayaya	Come all birds and share this sweet song
Agbonojo luka abaya sayọ	We've got a good visitor, rejoice with us
Ẹyẹ gbogbogi abalogo sayaya	Come all birds and share this sweet song
Agila palabawo abaya sayọ	Agila the magical one should rejoice with us
Ẹyẹ gbogbogi abalogo sayaya	Come all birds and share this sweet song
Naroko atitingbolo baya sayọ	Naroko the graceful mover rejoice with us
Ehingabọ luka baya sayọ etc.	Ehingabo the beautiful one rejoice with us etc.

Song Three

Ari isẹ jọkọ ka bi se lemora	I say a day's work can never tire me

Chorus– Ademora Jegbe, Jegbe ademora
Okun abadele ya ne mo owahangbogbo

Ari ise joko kabi sele mora

Ademora Jegbe, Jegbe ademora
Obade owa oba ilu hun mi
Ari ise joko kabise lemora

Ademora Jegbe, Jegbe ademora
Obade owa Etsu Musa keremulai
Arise joko kabise le mora

Ademora Jegbe, Jegbe ademora
Obade owa oile hun mi, oile
Kobi maki Dauda hun mi
Ari se Joko kabise lemora
Ademora Jegbe, Jegbe ademora

When you get to the great beyond
Greet everyone for us

and tell them a day's work never tires me.

When you get to the great beyond
Greet the past kings
And tell them a day's work never tires me.

When you get to the great beyond
Greet king Musa for me and
Tell them a day's job can never get me tired

When you get to the great beyond
Greet Oile the father of Maki Dauda and tell him a day's job never gets me tired

Song Four

Omaniri ko ni pono ejo
Omere ya etc

Little little snakes should give way
The big python is approaching etc.

Song Five

Oni mama no ni ama sabo oo
Chorus– Arayara ke saboraya
Ayalagbo mefa Ayaraya ke sabo oraya

Those who stand alone should come together
In togetherness, we shall protect ourselves
We of the six facial marks shall be together

Arayara ke	In togetherness, we shall
saboraya	protect ourselves
Ile ya noworo ayaraya kesa	At our homes in Oworoland
bo oraya o	we protect ourselves
Arayara ke	In togetherness, we shall
saboraya	protect ourselves
Egun leya sabo	With our masquerade we
oraya	shall protect ourselves.
Ayaraya ke sabo	In togetherness, we shall
raya	protect ourselves.

Truce with the Devil

For late Prof. David Cook who taught me that as a writer, I only need to answer to just two names, and I did just that.

Author's Note

This play can be called my first experimentation with a full length play which I was courageous enough to show to the legendary Prof. David Cook, the man who once taught the equally legendary Ngugi wa Thiong'o at the Makerere University in Uganda. Prof. David Cook was then taking me creative writing at the graduate class in the Department of English at the University of Ilorin. The play itself is a satire on the later abandonment of the creed of Marxism by its adherents; a kind of mockery of turncoat revolutionaries. The world of the play was heavily influenced by my close association with student unionism and some iconic figures of those heydays of students' populist struggles in my undergraduate days at the University of Jos. Many other characters in the play were influenced by their real life counterparts who crossed my path or whose paths I crossed in my search for meaning to life from the mid-80s to the early 90s. This was against the backdrop of the unravelling of the left, socialist thoughts and Marxist-Leninist creeds of that same period. It was a good setting for me to re-examine how far idealism can hold when faced with the realities of life. The student leaders of a bygone era are in focus in this play but we should ask, what are the students of this era doing in relation to societal populist clamour and where exactly are those great students' leaders of those bygone "golden age" of students' unionism?

Prof. David Cook did take a good look at my manuscript and in a full page foolscap typed script, pointed out the tentativeness of my construct and gave a rigorous analysis of what was not right with my experimentation; while laying out what I could do to solidify my "rapidly evolving literary/dramatic skills and vision." He wrote a very exacting critical commentary on this play on 28 April, 1993 and I hereby in 2014 share its world with readers and potential players; hoping that something useful will come out of it after all.

Abuja, January 2014

Dramatis Personae

Narrator

Suleiman	–	Student leader
Dapo	–	Fellow comrade
Kikelomo	–	A lady comrade
Old man	–	Suleiman's father
Uncle Yinus	–	Suleiman's uncle
Gbaguda	–	Uncle Yinus' gateman
1st Soldier	–	Guard of Kikelomo
2nd Soldier	–	” ” ”

Workers' leader

Striking workers	–	1st, 2nd and 3rd Workers

Crowd of students

Act One

Light falls on the stage. There stands the NARRATOR who faces the audience. He is about to tell them something.

NARRATOR: Ladies and gentlemen, you are all welcome to the realist theatre. Remember, this is a theatre of realism not escapism. If you wish to escape from painful reality by watching this play, then you have missed your way. Why not come out, claim your money and make it fast to the next brothel where people temporarily bury their worries in drinks and in the flesh of prostitutes? The play you are about to watch is a play of commonplace reality. I won't take much of your time because the cast are itching to come on stage. Our play for tonight is about struggle, struggle and more struggles! Meanwhile ...

(The NARRATOR is rudely interrupted by shouts off the stage. He strains his ear to pick out what the shouts are all about. He smiles knowingly.)

NARRATOR: Audience, let me tell you an open secret. The students are coming. They will never stop demonstrating against this and that. No to this, no to that. I bet you they will soon say no to God for creating this trouble-filled world. I take my leave.

(The NARRATOR scurries offstage and a crowd of students chanting war songs take over the stage. They carry tree branches and are stamping their feet on the ground. They start a new song.)

Today, Today
Tomorrow no more
If I die today, I will die no more.

Soli Soli Soli
Solidarity for ever
Solidarity for ever
Solidarity for ever
We shall always fight for our right.

(*The PRO of the Students' Union of the University of Jarasis,*
DAPO LADIPO, *mounts a raised platform to address the*
crowd.)

DAPO: Great Jarasite!

ALL: Great!

DAPO: Great Jarasite!!

ALL: Great!!

DAPO: Greeeeeaaaaaaat Jarasite!!!

ALL: Greeeeeeeeaaaaaat!!!

DAPO: I, Dapo Ladipo, hereby thank you all for listening to
the voice of the noble struggle against imperialism and
neocolonialism. We are at a crossroads in this country.
Our leaders are selling our land and resources to their
imperialist friends. The situation in the country is that of
misery, poverty, hunger, unemployment and tribulation,
all due to the shameless way our leaders sell the nation
to the imperialists and their agents. Let us not make a
mistake, this country is ruled by forces of neocolonialism
under the guise of financial institutions and multinational
companies. These multinational companies controlled by
USA, France, Britain, Japan and Germany are raping our
land relentlessly, and with the help of our servile leaders.
All these must stop if peace should reign in this country.
That is why we called you today. We will continue the
boycott of lectures until our demands are met. I now
call on Comrade Suleiman Shaku, the President, to give
the congress his address.

(*The speaker steps down from the rostrum and before the*

union president, SULEIMAN, can mount the rostrum, a
song in praise of him bursts out.)

ALL: Everybody shout Suleiman
Suleiman for us
We need Suleiman
Suleiman for us
We want, we want, we want Suleiman;
Suleiman for us.

(*The crowd of students are still singing when a frail-looking
student of average height mounts the rostrum. He wears a
brown caftan with a small skull cap to match. No watch
adorns his wrist and he has rubber sandals on his feet. He
raises his left hand to calm the singing crowd.*)

SULEIMAN: Great Jarasite!

ALL: Great!

SULEIMAN: Great Jarasite!!

ALL: Great!!

SULEIMAN: Greeeeeaaaaaaat Jarasite!!!

ALL: Greeeeeaaaaaaat!!!

(*The crowd says the third unionist's salutation
simultaneously with him, then they calm down.*)

SULEIMAN: Fellow colleagues in struggle. I believe you all
digested what the PRO has just said in your intellectual
stomach. Fellow colleagues, in fact you need not be told
that our leaders, or rather, rulers, are selling the country
to their imperialist friends. This is what every observant
and rational mind can see. It is the plight of most African
and third world countries under corrupt and reactionary
leaders. It is time we African youths saved the continent
from economic and political annihilation. The struggle
towards this goal must start here and now. It won't be
easy, my dear comrades, for a revolution does not happen
in a day. A revolution for political and economic liberty

must necessarily be watered and nurtured by sweat and blood, says a Yankee. This is the task before African youths.

Coming back to our own dear country, I believe you all heard the news that our leaders have taken the IMF loan, despite the rejection of it by the masses of this country. Not only that, they have introduced the dreaded and inhuman economic policy known as the Structural Adjustment Programme. To add insult to injuries, they have secretly signed an agreement with all multinational companies, which give the multinationals 60% shares to 40% government shares in all the big companies. What further proof do we need to see that we are about to be re-colonized by the devilish imperialists? Although we all rational students know that we have never really been independent. The only independence we got some decades ago was 'flag independence'. But, we all progressive forces in this country are battle-ready to stop this march to another slavery. All students in this country and workers through the central organ of the students and the workers have decided to start the beginning of the end of all neocolonialist and reactionary forces in this country. I am now calling on all students to go on indefinite boycott of lectures. The workers all over the nation would soon join us with their own weapons, strikes. Before then, we now give the zombie government 48 hours to rescind their devilish decisions of selling this country to the multinational companies and their imperialist friends.

We again call on the military zombies to go back to the barrack where they belong and let the people choose their leaders. Fellow colleagues, I swear with the collective power given to me that if the sit-tight zombies do not heed our ultimatum, which is from the people, then the streets of this country would be washed with the blood of all those against the people.

ALL: Yeah!

SULEIMAN: Great Jarasite!!

ALL: Great!!

SULEIMAN: Greeeeeeaaaaat!!!

ALL: Greeeeeeaaaaat!!!

SULEIMAN: Let us now move to the street and mobilize the workers and marketwomen. Please, don't attack anybody unless you are attacked. Expect the police and get set for the eventual struggle ahead.

(*Before* SULEIMAN *can come down from the rostrum, the crowd of students burst into songs of war.*)

ALL: Today! Today!!
Tomorrow no more
If I die today, I will die no more!

(*Lights fade as the students march off with their leaders. The* NARRATOR *comes back on stage.*)

NARRATOR: Suleiman was right! The stupid policemen did confront the students before they could get to the market-place. The students were determined to move on, and the police were also determined to earn their pay. Do you know what happened? Sure, I know you know. Well, if you don't know, just imagine what happens when a man with a gun fights another man wielding sticks and stones. The wielders of guns face the wielders of sticks and stones in an uneven battle, and believe me, there were casualties on both sides. It was a great battle. The workers could not join *en masse* as Suleiman thought. The government as usual threatened to sack any government worker that goes on strike, and replace him with those that are roaming the streets searching for jobs. The unemployed ones were eagerly waiting for the government workers to damn the government and listen to the voice of protest, so that they could be employed in their places as the government had said. After the government's fiery threat to sack and prosecute, some of the workers took a second look at the sunken faces of their dependants and relations. They wondered what would happen to those sunken faces if the jobs should go. Quietly, they tucked their tails between their legs and dashed the hopes of the unemployed ones.

We have forgotten Suleiman and his comrades. Their schools were shut, Suleiman and some others were expelled without trial, and some were rusticated. But that was not the end of the struggle. The die-hards believe that change will come when all arms wielded by the state will be useless against the armless but determined millions. They took solace in the fact that it has happened in the past, in some countries. Some comrades continued the solidarity and some couldn't withstand the strains. Eight years later, two old comrades met co-incidentally. Our play continues and *aluta continua!*

(*Exit the* NARRATOR *and light fades.*)

Act Two

(*Light comes on stage. Crowd of workers carrying placards and tree branches invade the premises of their company called African Trading Company. Their placards read: 'MONKEY DEY WORK, BABOON DEY CHOP'; 'WHO NO LIKE BETA THING'; 'OUR MONEY TOO SMALL'; 'NO PAY RISE, NO WORK'; 'LET MR CAPITAL DO ALL THE WORK'; 'WE MUST TO SHARE THE HUGE PROFIT'; etc. Somebody emerges from the crowd to address the workers. He is the leader of the workers.*)

LEADER: Great Workers!!

ALL: Yeaaaah!

LEADER: Great Workers!!

ALL: Yeaaaah!

LEADER: I salute you all!

ALL: Yes!

LEADER: I am happy that you heeded our call to embark on a strike action. Yes, we have been cheated for long. If you could remember the executive committee of the ATC workers' union tendered a letter to the administration calling for an increase in our pay. The letter was submitted to the personnel manager some four months ago, but up till this moment, nothing has been said about it. Who knows maybe the letter was used in cleaning their leaking anus?

(*Laughter rocks the crowd.*)

LEADER: Why won't their anus leak? It will leak because they have eaten more than their stomach can take. If you eat too much beans, na so so mess you go dey mess about.

73

(*Again the crowd laughs.*)

LEADER: Well, that is not the point. The manager and the rest increased their own salary and we ordinary workers were left to survive on the pittance called wages. We do all the dangerous work in the factories while they only read newspapers and fuck their secretaries and girlfriends in their offices. Later they will tell us that capital and entrepreneur are superior to labour. We are ready today to test this theory. We workers have now decided to leave Mr Capital to do all the work until our demands are met. Until then, no work for us. We have called for better working conditions and rise in pay. All our demands after due consultation with you the congress members have been submitted to the board of overfed directors.

"Who no like beta ting?" So says one of our placards. Yes we also like to ride air-conditioned cars to the factories and offices like the managers and the rest, instead of trekking or jumping from one bus to another to get to work. We like our children to attend good schools and feed well. We like our family to wear good and nice clothes. Yes, we like our wives to appear beautiful and attractive so that when we are at work, we will look forward to the happy night rest later in the day. So, fellow workers, the strike must go on. Well, let me now call on Mr Dapo Ladipo, a former student activist, to address you. He is very much involved in labour activities. Mr Dapo, come over.

(*The crowd gives way for DAPO to move on and soon he is on the table in the midst of the workers. DAPO raises a clenched fist and bellows.*)

DAPO: I salute you all workers!

ALL: We salute you, too.

DAPO: As your leader said, I am not a new person to labour activities. As workers, you should know that your greatest weapon is strike action. Workers have no other weapon than this. If it fails, then you become a butcher without a knife ...

1ST WORKER: Na true you talk, my brother.

(*Suddenly commotion erupts among the listening workers. DAPO is cut short in the middle of his speech. The workers have seen something of interest to them.*)

1ST WORKER: Here comes Mr Suleiman.

2ND WORKER: The yeye personnel manager.

1ST WORKER: So he dey for office na im we no mob am?

2ND WORKER: Na im and im assistant get mind to come office today when we dey strike.

3RD WORKER: That boy no dey fear!

(*SULEIMAN approaches the workers and they boo him. SULEIMAN disregards the boos, looking intently at the figure standing on the table. The figure, DAPO, is also looking at SULEIMAN as if he has seen a ghost. For a while, the workers are quiet and look at both men. SULEIMAN raises up his hands and shouts.*)

SULEIMAN: Dapo!

DAPO: Comrade Sule!?

(*DAPO jumps down and runs to where SULEIMAN is standing, a few metres away from the gathered workers. The workers look one another in the face and spring to attack SULEIMAN. SULEIMAN runs towards his office dragging DAPO along with him. Light fades on stage.*)

Act Three

(*Light falls on stage showing* SULEIMAN *panting on his executive chair.* DAPO *stands akimbo looking bewildered at* SULEIMAN.)

DAPO: Great Sule! Why are you panting like this? Is this the first time you will run such a race? Have you forgotten how we used to fly, hotly pursued by policemen?

SULEIMAN: Dapo, my long-lost comrade, what brought you here? This is a great reunion.

(DAPO *takes a long look around the tastefully furnished office, looks at* SULEIMAN *with eyes demanding for an explanation. He takes his seat in front of* SULEIMAN.)

DAPO: Is this your office?

SULEIMAN: Yes, Dapo, this is it.

DAPO: You mean you are the personnel manager of the African Trading Company?

SULEIMAN: That is true.

DAPO: Sule! This is the last place I expect to find you, holed up in here in the cavern of a capitalist corporation. I thought your sympathy lies with the workers.

SULEIMAN: Before I tell you my story, I would like to know how you got here.

DAPO: How I got here? I also have a lot to tell. I do some sort of work for the trade unions. I heard a lot about this company's attitude to its workers. When the workers here decided to embark on a strike action, they decided to contact me.

SULEIMAN: So you mean to say you're now a strike contractor or an itinerant troublemaker?

DAPO: Call it what you may. I take it as a duty to help the labour force and the progressive forces in this country.

SULEIMAN: Workers of all countries unite!

DAPO: But sure, I can't believe seeing you ... I mean look at where you are and what is happening outside. Tell me I am dreaming.

SULEIMAN: How can you be dreaming when you just led some hooligans into the company premises making some utopian demands?

DAPO: But they are your workers. They have the right to demand for better working conditions. Sule, where are all your Marxist theories and slogans? You who fraternized with the workers now calling them hooligans?

SULEIMAN: Yes. Who but hooligans do such a thing they intended to do to me outside? Did I hear you ask for my Marxist theories? Ah! Ah! Ah! ... I have burnt them all. Yes, I burnt all those books full of unrealistic dreams. Name them: Lenin, Marx, Engels, Plekhanov, Trotsky ...

DAPO: So you have been seduced by capitalism?

SULEIMAN: No, you got it wrong. I was seduced by reality after all those student days of sloganeering. My friend, let me tell you, I have stopped living on Marxist books. Marxism is dead, Communism has crumbled.

DAPO: Is that why no one heard about you? Many of us waited to hear from you but lost hope in continuing the struggle. I remained hoping to meet you one day. I thought that you have finally settled in the Soviet Union to study the way communism works just as you planned to do while we were faced with the harsh reality of expulsion and rustication. I cannot imagine seeing you on the cushioned side of the great divide.

SULEIMAN: Is it a sin to live well when the time comes?

DAPO: It was our effort then when we were in the school to make everyone to live well, but it was not this type of living-well that we were fighting for. You pretend to live well when the workers are outside itching to beat you to death. Sure, you now speak like a bloody capitalist ...

SULEIMAN: Have you just discovered?

DAPO: A tragic discovery indeed. I really demand to know what must have accounted for this great change.

SULEIMAN: You want to know? Fine, I will tell you.

DAPO: I just must know. Imagine? You ...

(A flashback to the past. Light fades on stage and scene changes to a room in a village environment. A slightly old but firm man sits in a sparsely furnished living room reading a newspaper with a funny-looking eye glass delicately perched on his nose. There is heavy coughing coming from the inner recess of the house. The man seems not to care. SULEIMAN walks impatiently out of the inner room and stands before the old man. He regards the old man for a time and speaks.)

SULEIMAN: Father, you seem not to care about Mama's sickness.

(OLD MAN *looks at him and shakes his head.*)

SULEIMAN: Will you continue to read old papers while Mama is dying? After all ...

(OLD MAN *drops paper and looks fixedly at* SULEIMAN.)

OLD MAN: After all what? After all, do I not understand things better than you? I sent you to the university, and you came back telling me that you have been driven back home ...

SULEIMAN: Father, I am tired of hearing this over and over again.

OLD MAN: Know that I am not tired of saying it. You now stand before me accusing me of not caring for your mother. Do you know how we suffered while you were in the university? Just at the time when we thought you will soon come out to give our bones some rest, you came back telling us that you have been sent away in the course of the struggle. What struggle? Don't you know I have been struggling all my life? When I left the civil service after 35 years with meager pension and gratuity, I came back to this village to struggle with unyielding farmlands. And you, who we sent to the university in order to ease our struggle with the pains of life came back to tell us you cannot continue because they sent you away in the course of the struggle. We sent you to learn. Who sent you to go and struggle with your teachers?

SULEIMAN: Father, you refused to understand. It is to prevent this kind of living that I chose the life I led in the university ...

OLD MAN: That is a lie! If you want to live well, you have to work hard. You do not seek for good living by causing trouble all over the place.

(*Dejection sets over the* OLD MAN's *face.* SULEIMAN *is still standing.*)

OLD MAN: I wonder why you chose to remain irresponsible. Sometimes I wonder what sins I have committed to be cursed with a son such as you. Look at how we have been living since I retired from the service. Look at your younger ones who had to leave school to help me in the dry farm since I cannot pay labourers. Your eyes are blind to all these, and you never come home except to roam the whole world in your ceaseless and fruitless struggle.

SULEIMAN: Father, why all these lamentations? Mother is

sick and you keep on blaming me. Am I the cause of the sickness? I have shown enough sympathy expected from a true son. What else can I do? There is no money to go to the hospital, and native medicine has not been working. What else can we do to save Mother?

OLD MAN: What else? I have tried all I can. What can the poor do but pray? Your uncle, who would have taken her to the hospital, deserted us because you called him a "bloody capitalist rogue".

SULEIMAN: Leave that out, Father! I still stand on my words. I will call him that again if necessary. He is one of those who feed fat on the labours of others and ...

(*They suddenly hear a torrent of ceaseless coughs from the inner room with muffled shrieks of little children. SULEIMAN and the OLD MAN dash towards the room. Light fades on stage just after a burst of a manly scream. The light comes on stage again showing SULEIMAN and DAPO looking into each other's eyes. SULEIMAN rises up and begins to pace the room.*)

SULEIMAN: That was how I lost my mother; my dear mum. She died an avoidable death all because of our poverty. We couldn't know what killed her; all we knew was that she was just so sick. After the incident, the old man shrank from life and became a living ghost. Our pathetic farm became more pathetic. I had to abandon my crazy ambition of writing revolutionary polemics. Remember the ambition we both had in the university of writing like Marx and Engels. I abandoned it midway to shift the struggle to the farm. It was not easy on that cursed farm, especially with the old man not doing much. Three years later, the old man joined the ancestors. It was as if the end of the world had come. I had younger brothers and sisters looking up accusingly at me with sunken eyes. Hunger reigned supreme in our home.

DAPO: It has been very hard for you just as it was with me. This life is a ceaseless struggle.

SULEIMAN: Yes, struggle, struggle, and struggle! I thought: what have all my years of identification with the "left" earned me? I asked myself, how long would I continue to mouth revolutionary jargon and slogans when calamities were happening around me, uninhibitedly? I knew then with the sudden family responsibilities placed upon me that I had to part with the illusionary world of struggle; of being an apostle of socialism.

DAPO: Oh no, don't say that ...

SULEIMAN: It was not my wish to say it, but I was forced by reality to say it. I looked round me furtively and all I saw were the sunken eyes of my younger ones. I knew I must do something. Here was only one way out of our misery: my bloody, capitalist, roughish uncle! I swallowed my pride and ran to him for help. He was willing to help seeing that hunger had broken my stubbornness. He lived in Lagos in a palatial building in Ikoyi. He mocked me before ...

(*Light fades on* SULEIMAN *and* DAPO *and falls on tattered looking* SULEIMAN *struggling with a gateman called* GBAGUDA *in front of a mansion in a highbrow environment.*)

GBAGUDA: You this hungry man, I say oga say make I no allow anybody come in. You no dey hear? If you no get job, make you no make me lose my own.

SULEIMAN: I am a relative of your oga. Just tell him Suleiman wants to see him.

(*The gateman looks at* SULEIMAN *with amused countenance.*)

GBAGUDA: Yeye! You wey your trouser tear for nyash like

this, na im you say you be oga brother.

SULEIMAN: That is not your business, just inform your oga that I am here.

GBAGUDA: I go show you say na my business to know who you be before you enter this place.

(*The gateman,* GBAGUDA, *pushes* SULEIMAN *out of the premises and at the same time muttering some obscenities. A plump man, bare to the waist emerges from the mansion fanning himself and smoking a pipe. He takes in what is going on and calls on the gateman.*)

UNCLE YINUS: Gbaguda!

(*The gateman turns round and stands at attention abandoning* SULEIMAN *who recognizes the man to be his uncle.*)

GBAGUDA: Yes, Oga. Na dis he-goat no allow me rest.

(UNCLE YINUS *looks at* SULEIMAN *properly and recognizes him. He removes his pipe and fans himself more vigorously.*)

UNCLE YINUS: Sule, what are you doing here?

SULEIMAN: I am here to see you.

(*Gateman shows surprise and withdraws.*)

UNCLE YINUS: That can't be, see me? Since when did cats and dogs become so friendly?

SULEIMAN: I apologize for what has gone wrong between us in the past.

UNCLE YINUS: Apologize? When have you, the fire-eating itinerant troublemaker turned to an apologist? Sense has finally entered your Marxist-ridden head. I know you will learn one day that words put on paper by insane people cannot get you a single meal. Just look at you. I knew you will come to me. The hungry look of your younger ones will surely force you. That I know. Why not run to East Germany or Soviet Union? Go to their embassies. They will give you a free flight ticket, since everything is free in their land, even women. Ah ah ah. I learnt their prostitutes do not charge money since everything is free. Imagine a life of free food, free cloth, free wine, free women and of course free men. Disciple of Marx, go to Russia and rush for a living!

SULEIMAN: I am only here for you to help my younger brothers and sisters ...

UNCLE YINUS: Have you forgotten? We capitalists are soulless. We have no soul, money is our soul. You cherish freedom and dictatorship of people like Gbaguda my gateman. Why not start mobilizing Gbaguda and others to take over this place. I bet you, hunger will soon dictate sense to your stomach just as it has now done. NO TO CAPITALIST EXPLOITATION, NO TO ECONOMIC SERVITUDE, NO TO MULTINATIONAL COMPANIES. YES TO REVOLUTIONARY FORCES. Those are your bogus slogans. I think it is time you shout YES TO HUNGRY STOMACH. Mr Revolution, is any revolution greater than the one going on inside your stomach? Ah ah ah ...

SULEIMAN: Stop this, Uncle. Why go into all these now?

UNCLE YINUS: I am happy you have learnt your lesson, thanks to hunger which knows no ideology, but you still need to learn. Gbaguda, take him to the boys' quarter and tell the cook to give him something to put into his ideological stomach. See me later tomorrow morning. My damsel must be waiting for me upstairs.

(The man walks triumphantly back into the mansion while GBAGUDA, wearing a condescending look leads the sullen-looking SULEIMAN to the boys' quarter. Light fades. Scene changes to SULEIMAN's office showing him pacing about while DAPO sits.)

SULEIMAN: That was how I entered into my uncle's capitalist trap. Just for the sake of my younger ones, I had to align with capitalism to survive. (SULEIMAN's *face brightens.*) Thanks to my uncle's numerous connections, I was able to finish my aborted education in a highly esteemed American university – Harvard. From there the world was virtually at my feet and I visited many countries.

DAPO: You became a capitalist globetrotter?

SULEIMAN: And I was opportuned to witness the forces of socialism by visiting communist countries. Lord, you know that while we were at school, I longed to see how the ideals of Lenin had been put to practice in Russia. Believe me, I saw the rich and the destitute in the so-called land of equals. I wondered where the socialist's creed of equality has fled to. I saw and heard the muffled oppression of the poor by the powerful. I saw that the poor and common of Russia were not happy with the leaders and with their own lives. I became disillusioned with socialism. It was then I realized that a classless society is a great illusion, and that man is inherently a capitalist. Dapo, it was when I came back from this trip that I burnt all the Marxist-Leninist books I own except the *Communist Manifesto* and Marx's *Das Capital*. I kept the two books for future reference and to remember the days I longed after illusion.

(DAPO *rises and joins* SULEIMAN *in pacing about the room.* DAPO *is at a loss of what to say.* SULEIMAN *sits and* DAPO *continues his pacing.*)

SULEIMAN: Dapo, stop pacing around like a one-legged hyena in the zoo. I have told you about my life as a capitalist. I got this job, again, through my capitalist uncle.

DAPO: I am at loss of what to say, so, you who do things for yourself, are now left at the mercy of a capitalist rogue like your uncle. Is that what you have been reduced to?

A pawn in the hands of vermins?

SULEIMAN: Venomous expletives won't help you. You are badly in need of a job.

DAPO: Me, in need of a job? Don't think you can give me a job in this filthy place. I am ready to starve for the rest of my life rather than serve capitalism.

SULEIMAN: Then what the hell do you want to do?

DAPO: I will continue to champion the cause of the workers, and I swear we will continue to fight renegades and traitors like you.

SULEIMAN: I reneged after seeing the truth,

DAPO: What truth? That the world was created so that some will remain perpetually poor and hopeless while others walk about with food-bloated tummies? That the strong has the God-given right to oppress and suppress the poor and powerless? Are those the truths you discovered? Slime!

SULEIMAN: Here you go again with those worn-out polemics.

DAPO: Whether worn-out or not, the truth and humanism of socialism shall prevail.

SULEIMAN: I am sick of arguments. Arguments are for frustrated people. We businessmen don't argue, we scheme. Now let us remember our friends.

DAPO: What friends?

SULEIMAN: Our comrades of course.

DAPO: What for?

SULEIMAN: To see how far they upheld the ideals of the dreams we had in school about the inevitable revolution. (*Smiles a mocking smile.*) Do you remember Kike?

DAPO: Which Kike? I don't know who you are talking about.

SULEIMAN: Have you forgotten her so soon, the one you love? Our little mummy? The mother of the struggle.

DAPO: You mean Kikelomo, my dear one? Our little mummy? The one we named the mother of the struggle?

SULEIMAN: Yes, the shapely beauty that followed the bunch of comrades. I saw Kike last month at the international airport on arrival from Washington.

DAPO: You mean you saw Kike? Did you talk to her? Did she ask of me? Oh, my Kike, after all these years!

SULEIMAN: Foolish Romeo, let me tell you about the new Kike. The Kike of the jeans, cap and t-shirt fame, the one you know, belongs to history.

(*Light fades and scenes changes to the arrival-departure hall of an international airport. All the usual activities in an airport are taking place. SULEIMAN appears at the arrival-departure hall in a suit, clutching a black briefcase. He sees a lady gorgeously dressed in a native attire with a larger-than-life head-tie to match. His eyes meet that of the lady and signs of surprise and recognition are exchanged between them. The lady is standing between two gun-wielding soldiers. SULEIMAN moves briskly towards the lady but is confronted by one of the soldiers while the lady looks on.*)

1ST SOLDIER: Na where you dey go?

SULEIMAN: What's your business?

1ST SOLDIER: Look this yeye man. As I see you dey waka go meet Madam like somebody wey shit don catch, you think say I no go ask you?

SULEIMAN: Piss off and let me see that lady.

1ST SOLDIER: Me to piss off? You know who you dey talk to at all? Even sef, you know who you dey rush go meet?

SULEIMAN: I don't care to know who you are and it is not your goddamn business if I know your madam.

(2ND SOLDIER *leaves Madam where she is now sitting unruffled and joins the struggling duo.*)

2ND SOLDIER: Musa, na wetin dey happen?

1ST SOLDIER: No mind dis bloody civilian. E for good make we go teach am sense for barrack. *Shege mutum!* He say he wan see Madam and I ask am wetin Madam owe am, so he take that im oversize mouth dey abuse me.

2ND SOLDIER: Mr Man, na so matter be?

SULEIMAN: I am not here to be questioned by any gun-wielding ragamuffin. I have the right to meet anybody. Remember this is a public place. It is not your barrack.

2ND SOLDIER: If na public place nko? They tell you say Governor wife na somebody wey you fit see for road and grab her hand or kiss fiam like that?

(*Madam suddenly springs from where she is sitting watching the argument and catwalks towards the arguing men. She taps the two soldiers on the back rapidly.*)

KIKE: Musa, Jaja, move aside.

(*The two soldiers give a salute and step aside. KIKE and SULEIMAN regard each other for some seconds.*)

SULEIMAN: Kike, is it really you?

KIKE: Suleiman, I can't believe seeing you in a designer's three-piece suit.

SULEIMAN: Why did you sit watching while those crude soldiers harassed me? By the way, what have you got to do with them or rather what have they got to do with you?

KIKE: They are my husband's guards. Don't you know I am no ordinary citizen? I am the First Lady of Santika State, which means I am the wife of Lt. Col. Lamidi Sanni, the Governor of Santika State.

SULEIMAN: (*Teasingly.*) Hmm, little mummy, mother of the struggle. Have you abandoned us your children? Have you ceased struggling for the masses?

KIKE: (*Suddenly furious.*) I am nobody's mother. Those chapters of my life remain closed for ever. I am Alhaja Kikelomo Olowo Saudi, an international businesswoman. I am on my way to Saudi Arabia, *en route* New York. Right now I have no time for long-time-no-see-talk. My chartered jet is waiting at the presidential lounge. Take this card. (*Gives him a card.*) You can see me in Santika Government House in a month's time when I come back. (*Smiles.*) Comrade Suleiman! It is nice seeing you again, and what a change!

(*She hurries off after calling the two bewildered soldiers to attention. They run after him while SULEIMAN looks on in surprise. Light fades. Scene changes to reveal SULEIMAN and DAPO in their former position before the flashback.*)

SULEIMAN: That was how I met little mummy on her way to the oil kingdom, with all the trappings of the wife of a notorious governor. I didn't bother to check her at her fortress if she was back or not. Should I give you the card so that ...

DAPO: What do you mean?

SULEIMAN: What do I mean? Were you not so eager to hear about her some minutes ago? Are you not her long-lost lover, eh? Don't you like to hold her hands once again?

DAPO: No, I don't! How can I wish to see her when she has betrayed the cause and didn't even remember me?

SULEIMAN: Remember you? Ah ah ah. You are funny. She is busy jumping from one plane to another. How can she remember you? To her, you belong to ancient history, like the dinosaur.

DAPO: I have never trusted women to persevere in the long march towards the revolution. They too much like the good things of life. But how could one know that Kikelomo or even Suleiman will later side with the oppressors?

SULIMAN: Look, fellow, let us not relapse into the former argument. Remember we still have some more friends to talk about.

DAPO: I am tired of your tales of betrayal!

SULEIMAN: But you must hear this one. Don't you remember Chukwudi, our in-house writer? The one who used to write out those fiery resolutions and releases? Nobody knew then that Chukwudi was in his own way getting ready for the pen-pushing profession.

DAPO: You mean Chukwudi is now a journalist?

SULEIMAN: Yes, a greedy one for that matter. I met him by accident after our annual general meeting with share-holders. Chukwudi was one of the numerous hungry journalists that covered the occasion for their papers. Do you know he couldn't recognize me? Maybe I have changed with this miniature potbelly (*Taps belly.*) but Chukwudi hasn't changed a bit. I can pick him out in a crowd.

DAPO: Then how did he meet you?

SULEIMAN: Ah, that was interesting. He was sent by his colleagues for the usual brown envelopes. I gave him a huge sum, since then, Chukwudi has been a regular caller here. He might walk in anytime from now.

DAPO: It is sad that most of the comrades have turned betrayers. They have entered into a truce with the devil called capitalism. They have betrayed the cause of progress and struggle. The other day I was taken to the police station for causing the kind of uproar taking place outside this office. I got to the counter and met Kilanko, the scourge of policemen, in uniform.

SULEIMAN: A policeman?

DAPO: Yes, Inspector Kilanko. Unlike you, he was ashamed of himself when he saw me. We couldn't say more than greetings to each other. He let me off immediately. Our meeting was indeed a sad and embarrassing one.

SULEIMAN: Let's us not go into any other embarrassing remembrance. But Dapo do you still reject my job offer?

DAPO: What job offer? I told you I can never work in this kind of establishment. Me work in a multinational company?

SULEIMAN: You are badly in need of a job. Look at your dress. It is not fitting for a man like you.

DAPO: Nobody is complaining, my dear well-dressed man.

SULEIMAN: But decency complains! It is time you reasoned and make better things out of life. Look, let us stop being idealistic, this life is real.

DAPO: There is nothing like idealism in wishing the poor and oppressed a better condition now. We want it now and not the future.

SULEIMAN: Now? You can't be serious. You are alone in your illusory world. The people you are hoping to lead are far behind you. All they need is a little satisfaction and not any grandiose satisfaction like a classless society.

DAPO: But you don't even give them that little satisfaction. I do not need to tell you about workers' hope. It is what you knew before you chose to forget.

SULEIMAN: I agree I once lived in your world. Now I live in the other world and you are yet to live in mine. That means I am more informed.

DAPO: Informed about what?

SULEIMAN: About where the realistic truth lies between your world and mine. Dapo, you know quite well that socialism's one basic belief is that no society is immutable to changes. Why have you, a man in society, refused to change? Today, socialism is no more, why are you holding on to the past?

DAPO: The socialist concept of change is that of progress. Change from the worst to the better. Your own type of change is that of retrogression and degeneracy. Do not twist socialist concepts to fit your capitalist ego.

SULEIMAN: I am not. What I am trying to tell you is that even the socialist blocks in the East have embraced capitalism. You preach your socialism as if you have never heard of the crumbling of socialism.

DAPO: What if socialism has crumbled? That would not stop my demand for a change of workers' condition in this society. This society and this system of ours need a crucial modification. There must be change, my good friend!

(*Suddenly they hear a flurry of stones hitting the door and breaking the window panes. They are startled. SULEIMAN gets up to peep. They hear the workers chanting "Dapo! You are a traitor, enemy of progress". DAPO turns to SULEIMAN.*)

DAPO: I have soiled my name by engaging in a dialogue with you. I am going out to explain myself to them.

SULEIMAN: Go out? They will kill you!

DAPO: It is good dying in their hands.

SULEIMAN: Don't be a hero. Wait till things get settled. Don't worry, the police are on their way.

(*The roar of a lorry comes to them. They rush in to peep. The anti-riot policemen jump from the lorry and descend on the workers with blank bullets, batons and tear-gas. DAPO rushes out of SULEIMAN's office and plunges himself deep in the midst of the workers. The workers look baffled by his sudden appearance. Then together they face the policemen. The policemen chase the workers and the workers chase the policemen. Light fades on stage with this background of confusion. Out of the rubble emerges the* NARRATOR.)

NARRATOR: Audience, you have seen great changes and great perseverance. Change and perseverance are two things that keep the world alive and interesting. Our play of tonight was concerned with these two things. The world is indeed a place of ceaseless struggle. Do not cease struggling, my people, for that tree in my backyard which ceased struggling awhile was felled by yesterday's wind.

Curtain.

Fringe Benefits

For my former students, former colleagues and friends: Johnson, Ben Ogbage, Charles Akpoyibo, Haliru Bala, Jibrin Hassan, Wasiu Ola-Awo, Mustapha Zubair and others who may or may not recognize themselves in this fictional world that bears resemblance to that citadel and fringes we all had dealings with.

Author's Note

This is a radio play written for the BBC African Performance drama competition in 1997. Another version of it was produced for the Women's Rights Advancement and Protection Alternative's (WRAPA) radio drama series against abuses of women and the girl child in 2005. Let me just say the play is an exposé on the happenings in our ivory tower in which I was then a participant-observer and leave the readers to come to their own conclusions.

Abuja, January 2014

Scene One

The background noise should indicate the hurly-burly of a lecture hall. A gradual silence descends on the room to show that the lecturer has just entered the lecture hall.

BANJO: Today we shall continue our study of the major literary critical theories. The critical theory we shall contend with this morning is Psychoanalysis. That is, we shall examine how literary criticism has been enriched by the theories of psychoanalysis. Before we go into the discussion proper, I will call on the three students that are expected to present short papers on this topic this morning, that is our kick off point. (*Ruffling of papers.*) Where is Augustine Wayas?

VOICE: Sir, Augustine is on admission in the hospital. He has typhoid fever. The water in the hostel is bad.

BANJO: And where is Hilda John?

(*Silence.*)

Now, she is on admission for what?

VOICE: Jungle fever.

(*General laughter.*)

BANJO: That's alright. Now where is Yaqub Mohammed?

YAQUB: I am here, Sir.

BANJO: That's right. Let us hear what you've discovered on psychoanalysis and literary criticism.

YAQUB: Sir, I have discovered nothing!

(*General laughter.*)

BANJO: Will you all keep quiet! If I hear any more of such stupid laughter, I will stop coming to this class for the rest of the semester.

(*Silence.*)

Yaqub, let me hear you again.

YAQUB: Sir, I have not been able to come up with anything.

BANJO: May I ask why?

YAQUB: I can't get any book in the school's library on the topic.

BANJO: Do you want to tell me that the topic is such a new one that nobody has written anything on it?

YAQUB: Honestly, Sir, there is nothing about it in the library.

BANJO: There is nothing or you are a lazy researcher? Do you even know how to use the library?

YAQUB: I passed my use of library course. It is the library that is the problem. The place is a museum. The books there are outdated.

BANJO: Well, I still believe you have not tried hard enough. Who amongst the rest of you has done an independent reading on the topic?

(*Silence.*)

Nobody? If that is the case then I will end today's lecture at this point. And let me tell you all one thing, I have resolved to stop spoon-feeding you. This is a higher institution not a primary school. If you are not ready to do some readings on your own, don't expect much from me. Tell Hilda John, the second presenter, to meet me in my office with her paper when she comes. Good day.

Scene Two

At BANJO*'s office. The nibbling of the keys in the keyhole and the opening and banging of the door suggest his entry into the office.*

BANJO: It is stuffy in here. (*Tries the control switch of the ceiling fan.*) Oh God! No light. I must open the windows. (*Tries the window panes. A knock is heard.*)

BANJO: Yes, come in.

(*The door opens and an old friend of* BANJO, CHUKS, *enters.*)

BANJO: Ah. It is you son of a dog! When did you hit town?

CHUKS: Just this morning and I decided to come immediately to pay homage.

BANJO: Come off it, this isn't the palace. If you want to pay homage, then hurry to the palace but don't forget to go with something ample for the royal fathers.

CHUKS: Royal fathers? To me they look more like royal idlers.

BANJO: Men, forget them. Have your seat. What's up, guy? Seeing you this morning means today is made. There must be news, and if there is no news, the coming evening will surely not be wasted.

CHUKS: You got it right. There is news, plenty of it, but the news should be better left till when we get to the club house.

BANJO: You are my man. Words of good tidings are best said with tongue well oiled by Bacchus, the wine god.

CHUKS: Hmm, trust you to wax poetical at the slightest opportunity.

BANJO: I teach poetry, I write poetry, poetry is my life. (*A knock is heard.*) Who the hell is that? (*The door opens and a girl,* HILDA JOHN, *enters.*)

HILDA: Good morning, Sirs.

BANJO: Morning.

CHUKS: Hello, young lady.

BANJO: You are Hilda I suppose?

HILDA: Yes, Sir.

BANJO: And why were you not in class this morning? You were to present a short paper.

HILDA: Sir, there was no water in the hostel and we had to wait for more than an hour for the tanker that finally brought us water. And ...

BANJO: Stop there. I have heard enough of students' problems this morning. I am a lecturer not the students' affairs officer. Is your paper ready?

HILDA: Sir, there is a problem. I couldn't get any book on the topic in the library.

BANJO: Same story like the others. And what other efforts did you make?

HILDA: I checked you twice in this office to see if I can get some books from you but you weren't around and I don't know your house ...

BANJO: Were you told I have a library at home?

HILDA: No, but I just want to see if I can get some books from you. Sir, can I get some books from you so that I can work on the paper before the next lecture?

BANJO: Funny indeed! You give an assignment, the students

end up borrowing books from you for the same assignment. Well you can see I don't keep books here. I packed all my books home since the office of the Prof. next door was burgled and all his books and research papers stolen.

HILDA: So, Sir, can I meet you at home this evening?

BANJO: If you wish. But you don't know the place.

HILDA: You can tell me.

BANJO: Well, it is Block A, Flat 7, the Senior Staff Quarters.

HILDA: Okay, Sir, I will be going, until I come.

BANJO: You are welcome. (*Sounds of clicks of the shoe heels on the floor as the girl leaves. The door opens and closes. A long whistle is heard from* CHUKS.)

CHUKS: Wow! That dame's front and back elevation is something! You guys here are such bloody opportunists! Just look at how that girl planned her way to your house and how you hurriedly swallowed the bait.

BANJO: That is what we daily face here. The man who can escape from the seductive ploy of that girl must be the Tibetan Dalai Lama himself.

CHUKS: But friend be careful o! The scourge is in town. I don't know how to write an elegy o, nor can I sing a dirge.

BANJO: Don't fret your life over me. These days I enter into combat with my sword fully sheathed.

CHUKS: I just hope one of your many combats won't ruin today's evening.

BANJO: Don't worry; she might come with a friend. And moreover it is not the day we harvest the corn that we brew the beer. The combat can take place any other day. Fringe benefits will always be there for the conscientious and tireless worker.

CHUKS: Fringe benefits indeed!

BANJO: You are a businessman, self-employed. You are in the mainstream; you don't need a fringe benefit. Fringe benefits are for those on the fringe like us, those who work for others. Working for others is not always that easy, that is why fringe benefits must come into the picture.

CHUKS: What a fringe benefit you have there.

BANJO: Outside here, getting such nice things cost money. You know about that better than I do. But here you daily get offered them or you seek them out yourself at relatively minimal cost.

CHUKS: Oh! I see, it is a case of an eunuch not suffering from two evils at the same time. If he is not potent downstairs, then he must have a large farm somewhere.

BANJO: You got it right. In the academics the financial potency might not be there, but there are available fertile lands to sow all kinds of oats.

CHUKS: Men, don't you think we should continue this discussion elsewhere; this office is getting too stuffy for me.

(*A knock is heard at the door.*)

BANJO: Whoever is there should come in quick.

(*Enters* HALI, *the publisher of a community newspaper, where* BANJO *is an editorial consultant.*)

BANJO: Oh, it is you, you are welcome, Mister Publisher. Have a seat.

HALI: Thank you.

BANJO: This is a friend, Chuks. Chuks, this is Mr Hali, publisher of *Grassroot*, the community newspaper.

(*Exchange of pleasantries.*)

HALI: Well, I won't be staying long. I just decided to breeze in and give you this (*Hands in an envelope.*), your honorarium for last month's edition. Work would soon commence on this month's edition.

BANJO: Thanks.

HALI: I will be going. There is no need to see me to the car since you have a friend with you. I will get in touch with you soon. (*Exits.*)

CHUKS: Hmm, this time a benefit from the fringe in physical currency. Tonight is full of promise. But you never told me you are now a journalist to boot.

BANJO: I do some hack-writing and some other jobs for his paper, and he pays me a labourer's wage beautifully named honorarium. Publishers are the same everywhere. I remember I once tried crossing to journalism, a profession that is my first love. I did a lot of its campus equivalent while I was in school. I got a job in one of the radical dailies in the Big City. I took up the job but I had to beat a tactical retreat back here. The workload is as heavy and hazardous as that of a donkey and the pay was horrible. Publishers always claim that their papers are not making much profit and the reporters slave away with the hope of becoming famous and landing a press secretary job to some big shots later.

CHUKS: It is hard for everybody these days; even we in the business world do not find it easy.

BANJO: Don't give me that crap. You people are in the mainstream unlike us fringers here.

CHUKS: So you think ...

(*A knock is heard. Enters a messenger.*)

MESSENGER: Oga, you get letters.

BANJO: Letters? Some of my much expected replies must have finally crawled here.

MESSENGER: Oga, na dem be dis.

BANJO: Thank you. Take this, take buy kola.

MESSENGER: Thank you, Sir.

BANJO: This letter here must be from my mother. The handwriting on the envelope looks like that of a professional village letter writer. (*Noise of envelope being opened.*) I got it right. (*Reads aloud to the hearing of* CHUKS *or the mother's voice can be used.*)

Dear son,

How are you and how is your work? It took me this long to write again because I could not get somebody who can write in English, since you told me to stop writing letters to you in our local language. Everybody who knows a little English here sees himself as someone of the city. I was lucky to get somebody this morning, a son of my sister, who has come to the village to visit his mother.

Son, my main aim of writing this letter is to remind you once again that it is time you think of getting married. You are not getting younger. Most of your age-mates are married with children. Remember you are an only son and I am a widow. Your sisters are all in their husbands' houses and I am alone. It is time you bring a wife home to me. You have never told me you are serious with any girl. The last time I visited you in the city, all you do is bring home different girls with bad manners and tell me they are your friends. If you can't find a decent girl to marry in the city, know that the village is filled up with them. I don't understand you, when you come to the village your behaviour shows you like the girls here but you have never considered any one for marriage. Is it the education thing? Some of them at least finished secondary school. Or is it money? Look, I have told you if the job you are doing cannot support you and a wife, you should find another job. Labourers and farmers here are married with children so I see no reason why a government worker like you should tell stories of not having enough to sustain a wife and children. I hope you are not giving away your money to those bad-mannered city girls?

I will stop here until I hear from you. Your uncle sends his greetings and everybody. And before I forget, Yemisi, that daughter of my good friend sends her greetings too. She is such a nice girl, she comes here almost daily to help me in the house. I wanted to send you some of those local spices you like so much but I was told I cannot send them with the letter. Bye bye for now. Take care of yourself. It is me, your mother.

CHUKS: Ah ah ah ... Your mother is damn funny. She wants you to spice your life with those local spices back in the village. Poor woman, she is yet to know that your appetite has been far too corrupted by modern delicacies all round you here.

BANJO: Don't mind her; all she wants from me is a wife. She will be the happiest woman alive the day I marry.

CHUKS: Why not make her happy then?

BANJO: Look at who's talking ...

CHUKS: Hold it. I might not be married but I have got a steady girlfriend and I will soon marry. Your mother is right, you need a steady.

BANJO: I don't need any steady. All I know is that when the time comes for me to marry, I will do so.

CHUKS: That's okay. You have forgotten the second letter. Maybe it is from your father in heaven, and probably on the same wife issue.

BANJO: You are not serious. Are you here to read my letters with me?

CHUKS: Remember we do the same whenever you come to my place.

BANJO: Okay, let's see what we've got here. (*Opens the letter, reads a little and shouts Hurrah! or other expressions of joy.*)

CHUKS: What, what is it?

BANJO: Take, read, man!

CHUKS: (*Reads.*) Eh! You've finally landed a job abroad!

BANJO: Yes, I am leaving this hell-hole for a place where what I do here will be better appreciated. What a day! (CHUKS *is silent and* BANJO *looks hard at him.*) Ah, it is like you are not happy.

CHUKS: It isn't that. I am just thinking, what happens to your mother, how will she take it?

BANJO: That is true. In my joy I have forgotten her. I will have to explain it all to her. I just have to take this job. Consider the opportunities it will open up for me. Remaining here after this offer will be self-punishment.

CHUKS: Just what will you tell the poor woman?

BANJO: I will tell her I just have to go. Is it not our people that say, "If one's fatherland does not make one's dreams realizable, then one would have to go elsewhere?" And I will not stay there forever. It is also our people that say, "No matter how sweet a journey can be, the sojourner will always return home." And to please her the more I can take a wife along with me or at least plant a seed before I leave.

CHUKS: That will be splendid! I can't wait for the evening. Why not let us kick off the celebrations now.

BANJO: Right here?

CHUKS: Of course, not here. We've got to scram from this stuffy place. (*A knock is heard.*)

BANJO: No, don't come in, we are on our way out!

The End

Kraftgriots

Also in the series (DRAMA) *(continued)*

Sam Ukala: *Two Plays* (2008)
Ahmed Yerima: *Akuabata* (2008)
Kayode Animasaun: *Sand-eating Dog* (2008)
Ahmed Yerima: *Tuti* (2008)
Ahmed Yerima: *Mojagbe* (2009)
Ahmed Yerima: *The Ife Quartet* (2009)
Peter Omoko: *Battles of Pleasure* (2009)
'Muyiwa Ojo: *Memoirs of a Lunatic* (2009)
John Iwuh: *Spellbound* (2009)
Osita C. Ezenwanebe: *Dawn of Full Moon* (2009)
Ahmed Yerima: *Dami's Cross & Atika's Well* (2009)
Osita C. Ezenwanebe: *Giddy Festival* (2009)
Ahmed Yerima: *Little Drops ...* (2009)
Arnold Udoka: *Long Walk to a Dream* (2009), winner, 2010 ANA/NDDC J.P. Clark
    drama prize
Arnold Udoka: *Inyene: A Dance Drama* (2009)
Chris Anyokwu: *Termites* (2010)
Julie Okoh: *A Haunting Past* (2010)
Arnold Udoka: *Mbarra: A Dance Drama* (2010)
Chukwuma Anyanwu: *Another Weekend, Gone!* (2010)
Oluseyi Adigun: *Omo Humuani: Abubaka Olusola Saraki, Royal Knight of Kwara*
    (2010)
Eni Jologho Umuko: *The Scent of Crude Oil* (2010)
Olu Obafemi: *Ogidi Mandate* (2010), winner, 2011 ANA/NDDC J.P. Clark drama
    prize
Ahmed Yerima: *Ajagunmale* (2010)
Ben Binebai: *Drums of the Delta* (2010)
'Diran Ademiju-Bepo: *Rape of the Last Sultan* (2010)
Chris Iyimoga: *Son of a Chief* (2010)
Arnold Udoka: *Rainbow Over the Niger & Nigeriana* (2010)
Julie Okoh: *Our Wife Forever* (2010)
Barclays Ayakoroma: *A Matter of Honour* (2010)
Barclays Ayakoroma: *Dance on His Grave* (2010)
Isiaka Aliagan: *Olubu* (2010)
Emmanuel Emasealu: *Nerves* (2011)
Osita Ezenwanebe: *Adaugo* (2011)
Osita Ezenwanebe: *Daring Destiny* (2011)
Ahmed Yerima: *No Pennies for Mama* (2011)
Ahmed Yerima: *Mu'adhin's Call* (2011)
Barclays Ayakoroma: *A Chance to Survive and Other Plays* (2011)
Barclays Ayakoroma: *Castles in the Air* (2011)
Arnold Udoka: *Akon* (2011)
Arnold Udoka: *Still Another Night* (2011)
Sunnie Ododo: *Hard Choice* (2011)

Sam Ukala: *Akpakaland and Other Plays* (2011)
Greg Mbajiorgu: *Wake Up Everyone!* (2011)
Ahmed Yerima: *Three Plays* (2011)
Ahmed Yerima: *Igatibi* (2012)
Esanmabeke Opuofeni: *Song of the Gods* (2012)
Karo Okokoh: *Teardrops of the Gods* (2012)
Esanmabeke Opuofeni: *The Burning House* (2012)
Dan Omatsola: *Olukume* (2012)
Alex Roy-Omoni: *Morontonu* (2012)
Chinyere G. Okafor: *New Toyi-Toyi* (2012)
Greg Mbajiorgu: *The Prime Minister's Son* (2012)
Karo Okokoh: *Sunset So Soon* (2012)
Sunnie Ododo: *Two Liberetti: To Return from the Void & Vanishing Vapour* (2012)
Gabriel B. Egbe: *Emani* (2012)
Shehu Sani: *When Clerics Kill* (2013)
Ahmed Yerima: *Tafida & Other Plays* (2013)
Osita Ezenwanebe: *Shadows on Arrival* (2013)
Praise C. Daniel-Inim: *Married But Single and Other plays* (2013)
Bosede Ademilua-Afolayan: *Look Back in Gratitude* (2013)
Greg Mbajiorgu: *Beyond the Golden Prize* (2013)
Ahmed Yerima: *Heart of Stone* (2013)
Julie Okoh: *Marriage Coup* (2013)
Praise C. Daniel-Inim: *Deacon Dick* (2013)
Wale Odebade: *Ariwowanye (The Uneasy Head)* (2013)
Soji Cole: *Maybe Tomorrow* (2013)
Wunmi Raji: *Another Life* (2013)
Sam Ukala: *Iredi War: A Folkscript* (2014)
Bashiru Akande Lasisi: *The First Fight* (2014)
Angus Chukwuka: *The Wedding* (2014)
Prince Ib' Oriaku: *Legend of the Kings* (2014)

Printed in the United States
By Bookmasters